ROUTLEDGE LIBRARY EDITIONS:
SOVIET ECONOMICS

Volume 21

THE SOVIET UNION LOOKS AHEAD

THE SOVIET UNION LOOKS AHEAD

The Five-Year Plan for Economic Construction

VARIOUS AUTHORS

Routledge
Taylor & Francis Group
LONDON AND NEW YORK

First published in Great Britain in 1930 by George Allen & Unwin Ltd

This edition first published in 2023
by Routledge
4 Park Square, Milton Park, Abingdon, Oxon OX14 4RN

and by Routledge
605 Third Avenue, New York, NY 10158

Routledge is an imprint of the Taylor & Francis Group, an informa business

British Library Cataloguing in Publication Data
A catalogue record for this book is available from the British Library

ISBN: 978-1-032-48466-2 (Set)
ISBN: 978-1-032-48634-5 (Volume 21) (hbk)
ISBN: 978-1-032-48638-3 (Volume 21) (pbk)
ISBN: 978-1-003-39001-5 (Volume 21) (ebk)

DOI: 10.4324/9781003390015

Publisher's Note
The publisher has gone to great lengths to ensure the quality of this reprint but points out that some imperfections in the original copies may be apparent.

THE SOVIET UNION LOOKS AHEAD

The Five-year Plan for Economic Construction

LONDON
GEORGE ALLEN & UNWIN LTD.
RUSKIN HOUSE, 40 MUSEUM STREET, W.C. 1

First published in Great Britain, 1930

Printed in the U. S. A.

CONTENTS

LIST OF DIAGRAMS

PREFACE

THE publication of the five-year economic plan of the U.S.S.R. by the Presidium of the State Planning Commission was preceded by a thorough consideration of the plan by the Congress of planning bureaus of the Soviet Union and by the government, and its ratification by the latter as the program of economic development to be followed in the period 1928-29 to 1932-33.[1] By way of introduction, the Presidium of the State Planning Commission deems it necessary to point out a few very general conclusions that may be drawn from the discussions that accompanied the preparation of the plan.

In the first place, there should be mentioned the complete unanimity of all the planning agencies of the country in their appraisal of the plan as drafted. All the essential policies embodied in the plan, in regard to the tempo of economic development in the various fields, the amount and the distribution of capital investments, the character of the program of capital construction, the general social and economic problems, etc., met, on the whole, with unanimous approval. This unity of opinion has been due to the fact that the plan successfully embodies the general directives given by the cen-

[1] For explanation of fiscal year, weights and measures, etc., see Appendix III.

tral authorities in regard to the development of the productive forces of the country through industrialization and through socialist reorganization of peasant economy, with a consequent strengthening of the socialist elements in national economy.

Secondly, running like a red thread throughout the period of the examination of the plan, is the unquestionable triumph of the idea of power development as a basis of economic planning and construction. The power basis of the plan has met with deep response and unqualified recognition both from the workers on the economic front and from the public at large. In this manner the present plan is confirmed as the logical successor to the plan of electrification which Lenin called the second program of the Party.

The third feature of special importance brought out by the discussions, is the unanimity in regard to the regional division of labor in the Soviet Union in the period immediately ahead. This is the first five-year economic plan submitted for the consideration of the country with the regional aspects worked out on a complete scale, and with a thorough analysis of regional and inter-regional problems of economic development. The variegated nature of economic life in the different sections of the Soviet Union and the great complexity of the problems to be solved in raising the economic level of backward regions and of the various nationalities that were oppressed under the czarist régime, is a matter of more or less common knowledge. The complete unanimity on this point, attained as a result of joint discussions with the representatives of all republics and economic regions, bears testimony to the fact that the socialist plan of economic development has been drawn up in conformity with the policy of the Soviet government in the matter of nationalities and on the basis of a rational combination of the interests of the Soviet Union as a whole and of the constituent republics and regions.

Special mention should be made of the tremendous interest with which the five-year economic plan has been greeted by scientific organizations and scientific workers generally. A socialist plan must and can be a scientific plan. The designing of a socialist plan of national economy is based upon the work of an extensive system of scientific organizations and investigators. At the same time, it opens to these institutions and scientific workers endless opportunities for the application of all the fruitful, advanced and revolutionary ideas at their command in all the important branches of science.

Finally, of utmost importance also is the unanimity on the planning front in the appraisal of the five-year plan in its relation to the present economic situation. The plan had to be considered and adopted in the face of economic difficulties of considerable magnitude, which have caused some persons even to question the expediency of adopting at the present time a plan for five years. The opponents of the plan have been untiring in proclaiming the incongruity between the formidable scope of the tasks assigned, both in regard to general development and to production, and the current economic difficulties. They may be reminded, however, of the similar clamor raised in 1920 in regard to the contradiction between the electrification plan and the economic situation of the country at that time. In fact, the only way to overcome the difficulties of the present situation, which reflect the transitional nature of the present stage of economic development of the Soviet Union, is through the strict enforcement of the present plan of great works and a socialist advance on the entire front.

PRESIDIUM OF THE STATE PLANNING COMMISSION (GOSPLAN) OF THE U.S.S.R.

FOREWORD

TO THE SECOND EDITION

The Realization of the Five-Year Plan

By E. KVIRING
Vice-Chairman of the Gosplan (State Planning Commission)

THERE can be little doubt in the minds of those acquainted with economic conditions in the U.S.S.R. that the rate of the economic development of the country in the immediate future will be far in excess of the pace set by the Five-Year Plan, and that the original Five-Year Plan will be carried out in its entirety in about four years' time. Therefore, it will be of interest to preface the second edition of "The Soviet Union Looks Ahead" with a review of the contemplated revisions in the Plan. Considerable readjustments in the programs for the most important sectors of the national economy have become necessary in view of the achievements of 1928-29 and the prospects for 1929-30.[1]

It is by no means a simple matter to prepare an exact plan for the development of Soviet economy. Thus far all preliminary plans over a period of years have underestimated the possibilities. The Five-Year Plan, as

[1] A table has been added on page 270 showing the details of the results of the fiscal year 1928-29 in various branches of national economy as compared with the Five-Year Plan; also the original and revised programs for 1929-30.

ratified at the Fifth Congress of Soviets, has been no exception.

This has been the case especially in respect to state-owned enterprises. It also applies to the estimates of the Five-Year Plan with regard to the collectivization of agriculture, which aims at the consolidation of millions of peasant holdings into huge farms.

The economic growth of the Soviet Union dates back to the period immediately after the world and civil wars, when the New Economic Policy was introduced. Some people attributed the success of Soviet economy during the first years of the reconstruction period to the fact that private capital was then given a new lease of life, and also to the fact that the government had rehabilitated the old industry inherited from the former régime. In 1926 the pre-war level was reached and the rehabilitation period came to an end, but Soviet economy still continued to forge ahead with great rapidity.

In 1927-28 large-scale state industries showed an increase of 18 per cent in the physical volume of production as compared with the preceding year. (Private capital is confined mainly to small-scale enterprises and is, therefore, of little importance in the industrial life of the country.) Such an increase would, of course, be considered a notable industrial achievement in any country. Nevertheless, it was considered insufficient to meet the needs of the Soviet Union, and the increase in production to take place in 1928-29—

the first year of the Five-Year Plan period—was set at 21.4 per cent. This plan might be criticized as unduly optimistic, but there is sufficient indication that it was absolutely justified. As a matter of fact, the plan was exceeded substantially, the physical volume of production of state industry showing an increase of 24 per cent during 1928-29, i.e., over 2 per cent more than originally planned.

The achievements of the second year, based on the results of the first few months, promise to be even more impressive. The Five-Year Plan estimated a 21-22 per cent increase in production during the year. But in the control figures (annual plans) for the year a gain of 32 per cent was specified.

In no other modern country has a similar expansion of industry taken place. According to figures published in the Report of the Committee of the President's Conference on Unemployment [1] the production of raw materials [2] during the period between 1922 and 1927 in the United States showed an average annual increase of 2.5 per cent; factory production—4 per cent, and freight operations a ton-mile increase of 4 per cent.

Mr. Walter Duranty, the Moscow correspondent of the New York *Times,* wrote in one of his cables as follows:

[1] Recent Economic Changes in the United States, p. 635.

[2] Including the output of vegetable, animal, forest and mineral products.

"Every economist understands what it means to increase the production of a large country even to the extent of only 10 per cent. The attempt to increase production 32 per cent seems to be lunacy."

We do not consider ourselves lunatics and we are firmly convinced that the current year will substantiate our contention that the plan is completely in accord with reality and that it will be fully carried out. The first six months of the year showed an increase of 29 per cent as compared with the same period of the preceding year.

The total physical volume of production of Soviet large-scale industries in 1929-30 will be double that of 1913, the peak pre-war year—also a record for modern industry. According to the Standard Statistics Company, the index of industrial production in the United States was 81.2 per cent in 1913 and 128.3 per cent in 1929, or considering the figures for 1913 as 100, the 1929 index of industrial production in the United States was 158.0. All indications go to show that the physical volume of industrial production in the United States will be less in 1930 than in 1929. At best, therefore, industrial production of the United States will show an increase of 58 per cent over 1913 as compared with an increase of 100 per cent for the Soviet Union.

In this connection the following facts should be recalled. It is common knowledge that Soviet industries suffered greatly during the period of World and civil wars. Industrial production in 1921 reached a total of only 25 per cent of the pre-war figures. In 1927 it reached a mark of only 104 per cent. Since that time the Soviet Union has been able to increase the figures for its industrial production to 200 per cent of the pre-war total.

Is the aforementioned planned 32 per cent increase in the growth of industrial production in accord with reality? What is the basis for this phenomenal growth? First of all, let us recall the great experience we have gained in planning our economy, and the fact that we have a thorough knowledge of our resources, economic possibilities and stocks of raw materials, as well as of our productive forces. This experience furnishes the basis for undertaking this huge program.

I recall a conversation with Colonel Cooper, consulting engineer on the "Dnieprostroy" hydro-electric project. Whenever our engineers would ask him the reason for advising certain working methods, his answer would invariably be: "Because this is the American experience—such is usually the practice in American construction projects." This argument was inadequate for our engineers; for Colonel Cooper, however, it was decisive. In the same way, we may say that our planning experience gained during recent years is sufficient proof to us that our plan of a 32 per cent increase in industrial production during 1929-30 is based on reality.

Then, again, some may ask, Why should there be a further increase of 10 per cent over the increase estimated in the Five-Year Plan? What are the new factors of which we were not aware in the spring of 1929 that justify us in planning this increase in production? First of all, the basic reason may be found in the introduction of the uninterrupted work-week in industry,—which immediately increased industrial production with the aid of some increase in labor power, of which there is no shortage in the Soviet Union.

This one measure alone will result in growth of 6 per cent in industrial production in 1929-30, which was not anticipated in the Five-Year Plan. Furthermore, we are preparing a considerable increase in our plant construction during the year which will make available for operation more new and renovated plants than were contemplated in the Five-Year Plan. These are two basic factors which justify our raising the estimate of the Five-Year Plan by 10 per cent.

In 1928-29 the sum invested in state industry was 1.68 billion rubles. For 1929-30 this investment is to reach a total of 3.66 billion rubles, which means a more than two-fold increase in comparison with last year and 1.33 billion rubles in excess of the original figures of the Five-Year Plan for the year. These 3.66 billion rubles will be made up chiefly of the accumulated savings of Soviet industries, to the amount of 3 billion rubles. Thus, other branches of the national economy will be called upon to contribute only a few hundred million rubles towards the industrial construction program. Construction is confined chiefly to the heavy industries. Aside from reserves not yet allocated between the different branches of industry, there will be the following distribution of funds invested:

Heavy industries	2,754	million rubles
Light industries	449	" "

As far as the chief industries are concerned, these amounts will be distributed as follows:

Fuel Industry (coal, oil, peat)	557	million rubles
Metal Industry	990	" "
Building Materials	275	" "
Lumber Industry	200	" "
Chemical Industry	294	" "
Textile Industry	192	" "
Other Construction Projects	380	" "

What is the significance of the investment of more than 3½ billion rubles in industry, from the point of view of the realization of the Five-Year Plan? I have already mentioned that the capital investments for the first year of the Five-Year Plan amounted to 1.7 billion rubles. This gives total capital investments of over 5 billion rubles in the first two years of the Five-Year Plan, while we had not anticipated investing more than 13½ billion rubles in state industry for the entire five-year period. The fact that our capital investments could reach a total of over 3½ billion rubles in the second year goes to prove that not less than 5-6 billion rubles of capital investments will be made in industry in 1930-31. It is apparent, therefore, that our capital investments for the first three years of the Five-Year Plan will total about 10 billion rubles. There will remain the amount of 3½ billion rubles to be invested in the course of the fourth year in order to complete the schedule of the Five-Year Plan. From the achievements of the first two years it is clear that the volume of construction laid down in the Plan will be carried out in four years.

Let us compare the volume of capital investments planned for the coming year with that of previous years. For the entire period of 1923-1928 our total capital investments in state industries amounted to 3½ billion rubles. Thus our capital investments in 1929-30 will amount to as much as the total investments for the preceding 5 years. On the basis of such figures, the scepticism and criticism of two years ago leveled at our seeming audacity in starting such gigantic enterprises as the Dnieprostroy, has vanished. Now no one is surprised when the plan of the Gipromez (State Institute for Planning Metal Works) for the industrial development of the Dnieprostroy region calls for the construction of gigantic factories which will require more electrical energy than the Dnieprostroy can supply. Because of this Gipromez is already mapping out a program for additional power plants to make good this deficiency.

I will refrain from enumerating all the projected mills and factories and will confine myself to giving a few figures. According to the construction program (I list here only those projects that exceed 15 million rubles in value), 27 new factories will be erected at a cost of 15-20 million rubles each, with a total cost of 520 million rubles; 13 factories to cost between 30-50 million rubles each and a total cost of 500 million rubles; and 23 factories to cost more than 50 million rubles each at a total cost of 2½ billion rubles, or an average expenditure of 100,000,000 rubles each.

In the construction of these industrial giants, as well as in the colossal capital investments in all other branches of national economy, we are confronted with the very serious problem of organizing our construction activity on a new basis, in accordance with the latest achievements of world technique. This fact raises the problem of the necessity of securing specialists in the various branches. Next comes the problem of the mechanization of construction activity, which will require, first of all, the import of construction machinery on a huge scale and, at the same time, the development of our own machine construction and building industry, on which depends the rapid development and execution of the construction projects.

We are well aware of the difficulties of our tasks and realize also that our own forces are insufficient.

Therefore, we are planning to call to our assistance numerous foreign specialists and foreign construction firms, in order to organize our building industry, in the shortest possible period of time. The speedy construction of the contemplated factories is of the utmost importance in increasing the rate of industrial production. As an instance of this let us take the production of tractors.

According to the Five-Year Plan, it was anticipated that the tractor factory at Stalingrad would be completed by 1931, in order to be ready to start production during the last year of the Five-Year Plan. It was also planned to start the construction of a second tractor plant at Cheliabinsk in 1930, so that it could be completed by the last year of the period. The introduction of foreign specialists, the placing of large orders for construction materials in America, enabled us to speed up the construction of the Stalingrad plant greatly, so that instead of being completed by 1932 the factory will be ready for work in 1930 and will turn out tractors by the end of the summer of this year.

The success attained in speeding up the building of the Stalingrad tractor factory raised the question of accelerating the construction of other tractor plants. The government decided to start work immediately on the construction of two more tractor factories; one at Cheliabinsk with an annual production capacity of 40,000 fifty-horse-power tractors, and one in the

Ukraine with a yearly capacity of 50,000 thirty-horse-power units. The time limit set for the construction of both these factories was two years, and fifty million rubles was the amount assigned in each case for the construction program of the first year. This will result in a total of 700,000 ten-horse-power tractor units in the country by the end of the five-year period, instead of 180,000 as originally contemplated. In addition, tens of thousands of tractors will be imported during the next few years. Our own annual production will provide 400,000 units instead of the 100,000 indicated in the original plans.

Such an enormous growth in the production of tractors will have a tremendous influence on the development of agriculture and especially on the process of collectivization. The development of the tractor resources of the country will require a corresponding increase in the output of oil. Preliminary figures show that the contemplated output of 26,000,000 tons will be increased to 40,000,000. Such an increase over the original figures is of tremendous significance.

In all the most important branches of industry the Five-Year Plan estimates are being exceeded. We have reason, therefore, to be fairly certain of the completion of the Five-Year Plan in four years.

Our chief shortcoming in this process of development is the high cost of production. Hence, our plans for next year aim at organizing both the financial and the production side of our construction program in such a manner as to make it possible to complete huge factories costing tens of millions of rubles in two years' time; whereas only very large factories, costing hundreds of millions may take three years, or at most four years, for completion.

Let us now turn to the question of agriculture. According to reports of a news telegraph agency, Oswald Garrison Villard, editor of the "Nation" stated: "The Soviet Government has the hardest nut to crack in the peasant problem." This is certainly correct, but even this nut can be cracked. Our agriculture lags behind industry, and it should be stated here without equivocation, that in its present condition it is not able to keep up with the huge state industries for the simple reason that until very recently agriculture was confined mainly to very small peasant holdings. We were confronted with 26,000,000 peasant holdings. Such holdings could not become the basis for the rapid growth experienced in industry and therefore constitute the main difficulty to be overcome in the development of agriculture.

Agriculture must be extensively mechanized. This is an essential requirement in the Soviet Union, as well as in all modern countries. It is a well-known fact that in the United States the process of the rapid mechanization of agriculture has been going on for the past ten years. Tractors and combines are the chief factors in large-scale agricultural production with, of course, the electrification of the entire industry. In countries with a system of private economy this process results in the gradual absorption of the small holder by the big enterprise. In the Soviet Union it leads to a strengthening of socialist construction—to the growth of collectives, tractor service stations and large-scale state farms. Collectives constitute an important factor in the socialist reconstruction of agriculture; they aim at bringing about a gradual consolidation of poor peasant holdings into huge productive units. For the poor peasant this is the best means of improving his material condition.

The question arises, however, whether the masses of the peasantry will be willing to join the collectives. In this connection it must be borne in mind that the Soviet peasant differs very much from the average American farmer. In the Soviet Union small peasant holdings predominate. The area under tillage in 1929 comprised a total of 117,000,000 hectares, while there were 25,000,000 peasant holdings. From this the reader will obtain a fair picture of the size of such holdings. Only about 5 per cent of them belonged to "kulaks" (rich peasants). There is no possibility for the great masses of the small and middle Soviet peasants to find an outlet from their present low economic state except by the road to the collective. Only through collectivization based on large-scale production is it possible for them to escape from the poverty to which they are condemned as independent producers.

During the past two years there has been a great development in the collectivization of agriculture, and based on last year's success of the collective movement we are planning to bring 8,000,000 peasant holdings into collectives during the year, which will comprise about 30 per cent of all peasant holdings. Here too, the plan will no doubt be considerably exceeded.

The sown area of the collectives in 1929 was 4,300,000 hectares; this area was increased more than tenfold in 1930, amounting to about two-fifths of the total area under cultivation. To this should be added more than three million hectares of state farms and several million hectares of the tractor service stations. Already this year we expect to realize from the socialized sector 50 per cent of the marketable grain production of the country. This will be considerably more than the grain procured hitherto from 10 per cent of the wealthiest farmers. Hence by next year the socialized sector will become the decisive factor in agriculture.

This rapid growth of the collectives is far ahead of the Five-Year Plan, which was based on a very conservative figure and proposed to collectivize by 1932-33 (the last year of the period) about 15 per cent of the peasant holdings, with a sown area of about 21,000,000 hectares. These figures have been far surpassed already in the second year of the period. The great process of reconstruction which is taking place at present in the Soviet village leads us to believe that in the course of two more years the bulk of the Soviet peasantry will be collectivized.

The peasant problem is the hardest problem in socialist construction, but we are confident of solving even this problem. Large-scale collectives, uniting under a single administration thousands of small individual holdings and together with this the organization of large-scale state farms, are the means of solving the problem of socialist construction in agriculture. We will encounter great difficulties in the task, but the most important have already been overcome. The peasant masses—about 90 per cent of the poorer and middle peasants—already realize that the only way out for them is the large-scale collective, using the most modern agricultural machinery.

The rapid development of collectivization is meeting with opposition on the part of the richer peasants ("kulaks"). However, the tremendous growth of the state farms and of the collectives is making good the loss due to the reduction in the output of the kulaks. The basic problems of food supply in the Soviet Union have already been solved.

The rapid development of collectives and of Soviet State farms will remove all our difficulties in the course of the next few years and will result in an unheard of expansion of agriculture. On the basis of these attainments we are certain that not only in agriculture will our collectivization plan be exceeded, but also that the plan for agricultural production will be exceeded and the food conditions of the country thus materially improved.

It would require too much time to deal here with the other branches of our national economy. I will merely refer to the fact that in transportation, in trade turnover, and on the cultural front, just as in every other activity we are making big strides and are far ahead of the Five-Year Plan. We therefore entertain no doubts as to the realization of the plan.

In conclusion I wish to refer again to what Mr. Villard wrote about the Five-Year Plan. He said: "They worked out a gigantic, grandiose plan for the development and industrial rehabilitation of the country, and if they can be criticized it is only because they are going too fast and because their construction is ahead of their needs." In my opinion history will not criticize us for forging ahead too rapidly with our plans, but rather for not keeping pace with reality; it will criticize us not because our construction is ahead of our needs, but because the opposite is the case; because our construction is not sufficient to satisfy the growing demands of a people engaged in building up a socialist society.

May, 1930.

THE SOVIET UNION
LOOKS AHEAD

CHAPTER I

INTRODUCTION

THE five-year plan of economic development of the Soviet Union was prepared by the State Planning Commission of the U.S.S.R., in accordance with general directives given by the government, and in pursuance of the following general objects: carrying out of the policy of industrialization of the country, socialist reorganization of agriculture, and the gradual extension and strengthening of the socialist elements in the economic system of the country.

To the State Planning Commission and to the entire system of planning bureaus was assigned the task of translating these politico-economic directives into concrete technical and economic plans and calculations and of reducing them down to a program of economic development for the impending five-year period.

The present five-year program has been drawn on a scale far exceeding the scope of any previous plans, in regard to growth of the volume of production, capital investments, and to improvements in efficiency. This is a result, on the one hand, of the experience acquired during the early years of economic reconstruction, which brought out many potentialities formerly underestimated, and, on the other, of certain modifications in the nature and in the methods of planning work for the five-year period. In conformity with the instructions of the government to give the preparation of the plan a more public character, and also in order to secure expert scientific advice on the most important aspects of the plan, a number of special conferences, attended by scientists and practical experts, were held for the discussion of problems relating to metallurgy and machine construction, reconstruction of agriculture, reorganization of transportation, the chemical industry, wood distillation, the textile industry, small trades, co-operative development, training of a skilled personnel, and local enterprises.

On the basis of these conferences, and also of the extensive investigations conducted by a number of government departments and, in particular, by the Supreme Council of National Economy and the People's Commissariat for Transportation, it has been possible to draw up a sufficiently concrete plan of new construction designating specific projects, locations, and time limits, and also a program of reconstruction and rationalization in the leading branches of national economy. All estimates in the plan in regard to the rates of expansion in volume or of improvements in efficiency are based on these programs. From the methodological standpoint this procedure was of advantage in that it permitted dispensing with the method of extrapolation, which had to be employed in all previous planning work and which resulted in an underestimation of the potential rates of development.

At the same time, the State Planning Commission held a number of special conferences with representatives of the principal economic regions of the country. The actual resources and the potentialities of each region were thus considered from every angle with the direct participation of local people, both from the standpoint of the national objectives to be attained in a given region and of its specific characteristics and needs. The work accomplished by these conferences affords the possibility of presenting for the first time the principal elements of the five-year plan in their regional aspects. It has also permitted the obtaining of a general view of the problem of redistribution of productive forces between the various regions, as well as the special problems of the development of backward regions, to which specific attention has been drawn by the government instructions.

Finally, the work on the five-year plan has made it possible to study more intensively such synthetic problems as national income, the process of socialization, the balance of production and consumption of mechanical power, etc.[1]

[1] The English translation of the five-year plan contains only the maximum variant of the plan as adopted by the Congress of Soviets of the U.S.S.R. The original plan was drawn up with two variants, the so-called "basic" and "maximum" variants, representing the lower and upper limits of the program for every branch of economy. Since the Soviet Government has adopted the maximum plan as the goal for the five-year period, it has been con-

sidered advisable to omit the minimum program in the English translation.

In the minimum plan the total capital investments in national economy for the five-year period were estimated at 57.4 billion rubles as compared with 64.6 billion rubles in the adopted plan. The increase in industrial production for the period was put at 108 per cent for the minimum plan as against 136 per cent for the maximum, while agricultural production was estimated to show an increase of 44 per cent as compared with 55 per cent.

In Appendix I is contained a short description of the system of economic planning in the Soviet Union. An explanation of some of the terms and measures used in the book will be found in Appendix III.

Data on trade between the United States and the Soviet Union and on the technical assistance contracts concluded by Soviet organizations with American firms will be found in Appendix IV.

CHAPTER II

GENERAL SUMMARY OF THE ECONOMIC CONDITION OF THE SOVIET UNION

THE great task set by the five-year plan for the development of the productive forces of the Soviet Union, through rapid industrialization and steady strengthening of the socialist elements in national economy, is that of attaining and surpassing the economic level of the advanced capitalist countries in the approaching historical period, and of thus assuring the triumph of the socialist economic system. Accordingly, the scope and the rate of economic development in the Soviet Union must be measured not by a comparison with the miserable economic condition of Czarist Russia, but by the standards of economic and cultural progress which obtain in the most advanced countries of the modern world. The object must be, with the aid of the colossal natural resources of the Soviet Union, the advantages afforded by its system of an organized and planned national economy, and the latest technical achievements, to secure a rate of economic development higher than that yet attained by modern capitalist countries.

This does not, however, rule out the necessity of giving, by way of introduction to the plan, a very general analysis of the preceding stage of economic development, and a summarized comparison of the present level of the productive forces of the Soviet Union with that of pre-war Russia. While the significance of such comparisons is limited (especially considering the questionable accuracy of the estimates for 1913), they, nevertheless, bring out clearly both the achievements of the Soviet Union in the reconstruction period which has elapsed and those weak points in the economic system which must be remedied if the development of socialist economy is to progress successfully.

The memory is still alive of the disastrous effects of the World and civil wars upon the productive forces of the country. It is unnecessary to recall the wrecked condition of economic life in the country at the conclusion of the civil war, which ended in a crushing defeat for the united forces of Russian bourgeois and feudal reaction and its allies in Western Europe. Industrial production had fallen to 20 per cent of pre-war and agricultural production, to 54 per cent. The output of mineral fuels and of metal ores had stopped almost completely. The number of workers had decreased to 60 per cent of pre-war, and real wages amounted hardly to 35 per cent. The transportation system was serving almost exclusively military requirements, and economic relations between the various regions were completely wiped out. The market had disappeared and the monetary system had been destroyed. The terrible famine of 1921 came as an additional blow to the disorganized economic system of the country.

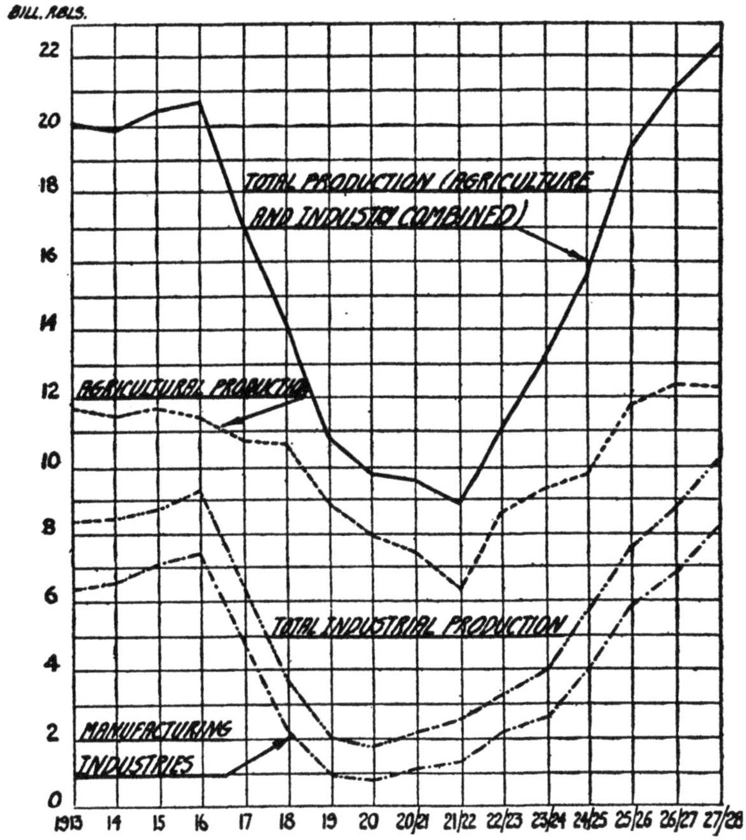

GROSS PRODUCTION OF THE SOVIET UNION
(In Billions of Rubles at Pre-War Prices)

The most sanguine optimists did not anticipate a restoration of the national economy to the pre-war level before 1930. However, the tremendous efforts of the masses of workers and peasants, who had carried the great civil war to a victorious conclusion, a correct economic policy, and the iron will of the proletariat, assured the completion of the rehabilitation period in a much shorter period. By 1927-28 the country had surpassed the pre-war economic level and had started on the road of basic reconstruction. The decline and the subsequent advance of the productive forces of the country are shown by the diagram on page 9, and by the following table. These figures afford a vivid illustration of the great tasks of the rehabilitation period:

GROSS PRODUCTION OF THE NATIONAL ECONOMY OF THE SOVIET UNION

(in billions of rubles at pre-war prices)

Years	All Industry	Manufacturing Industries	Agriculture	Total Production	Ratio to 1913 (Per Cent) Industry	Agriculture	Total
1913	8.43	6.39	11.61	20.04	100.0	100.0	100.0
1914	8.43	6.43	11.36	19.79	100.0	97.8	98.8
1915	8.66	7.06	11.75	20.41	102.7	101.2	101.8
1916	9.22	7.42	11.50	20.72	109.5	99.0	103.4
1917	6.38	4.78	10.72	17.10	75.7	92.3	85.3
1918	3.66	2.16	10.62	14.28	43.4	91.5	71.3
1919	1.95	0.95	8.86	10.81	23.1	76.3	53.9
1920	1.72	0.82	8.00	9.72	20.4	68.9	48.5
1920-21	2.08	1.08	7.42	9.50	24.7	63.9	47.4
1921-22	2.54	1.44	6.31	8.85	30.1	54.4	44.2
1922-23	3.33	2.13	8.54	11.87	39.5	73.6	59.2
1923-24	4.05	2.59	9.28	13.33	48.0	79.9	66.5
1924-25	5.65	3.96	9.75	15.40	67.0	84.0	76.8
1925-26	7.58	5.72	11.76	19.34	89.9	101.3	96.5
1926-27	8.76	6.72	12.37	21.13	103.9	106.5	105.4
1927-28	10.08	8.14	12.26	22.34	119.6	105.6	111.5

Along with these very general indicators of the economic development, the following table shows the great changes that have taken place in the economic structure of the country since 1913, and, at the same time, also points out some of the weak spots which have to be remedied in order to insure the uninterrupted growth of socialist construction.

	Unit	Amount 1913	Amount 1927-28	Ratio of 1927-28 to 1913 (Per Cent)
I. *Output of Electric Power*	millions of kwh.	1.945	5.050	259.6
Of which central stations	millions of kwh.	690	1,870	271.0
II. *Fuel*				
Coal	millions of tons	28.9	35.4	122.5
Petroleum	millions of tons	9.3	11.6	124.7
Peat	millions of tons	1.6	6.9	431.3
III. *Machine Construction*				
Internal combustion engines ...	1,000 hp.	26.5	106.9	403.4
Agricultural machines	millions of rubles at list prices	67	125	186.6
IV. *Metallurgy*				
Iron ore	millions of tons	9.2	5.7	62.0
Pig iron	millions of tons	4.2	3.3	78.6
V. *Chemical Industry*				
Soda	thousands of tons	154	205	133.1
Superphosphates ..	thousands of tons	55	150	272.7
VI. *Items of General Consumption*				
Cotton fabrics	millions of meters	2,250	2,742	121.9
Woolen fabrics ..	millions of meters	95	97	102.1
Granulated sugar..	thousands of tons	1,290	1,340	103.9
VII. *Agricultural Production*				
Grain	millions of tons	81.6	73.1	89.6
Cotton, unginned.	thousands of tons	744	718	96.5
Flax, fiber	thousands of tons	454	248	54.6
Sugar beet	millions of tons	10.9	10.1	92.7

A study of this table brings out five fundamental facts, which are of decisive importance for the entire national economic development.

In the first place, there is the tremendous expansion of power resources and of machine construction. The production of coal in 1927-28 amounted to 122.5 per cent of the 1913 production, that of petroleum to 124.7 per cent, peat—431.3 per cent, electric power—259.6 per cent, internal combustion engines—403.4 per cent, agricultural machinery—186.6 per cent. This is clear evidence of the fact that new construction work of great magnitude was started while the rehabilitation process was still under way.

A second fact to be noted, which looms as a serious handicap to the further progress of industrialization, is the failure to restore the iron industry to even nearly the pre-war level and its lagging far behind the growth of machine construction and the general requirements of the national economy. In the year 1927-28 the production of iron ore was 62.0 per cent of the 1913 production, manganese ore—56.6 per cent, pig iron—78.6 per cent, steel ingots—95.2 per cent, and rolled shapes—91.4 per cent. This is one of the central points in the whole scheme of economic development, and it demands the most assiduous attention. As will be shown later, enormous efforts and resources will be provided by the five-year plan in order to remedy this situation.

Another group of important problems relates to the

production of manufactures for consumption. For a number of the most important products, the 1927-28 production has considerably surpassed that of 1913, the ratio of the former to the latter being 121.9 per cent for cotton fabrics, 102.1 per cent for woolen fabrics, 103.9 per cent for granulated sugar, 116.3 per cent for salt, 132.1 per cent for rubber shoes. The growth of production, however, though proceeding at a faster rate than the increase in population, has been insufficient to meet the rapidly growing demand of the last years and, as a result, a shortage of consumption goods has developed. Proper attention must be given this group of industries, with a view of eliminating this shortage and of considerably increasing the consumption of manufactured goods.

A fourth point is in regard to industrial crops, which, although showing considerable expansion in recent years, still fall short of the developing needs of industrial production. The total area sown to industrial crops in 1927-28 was 132.7 per cent that of 1913. The yield per acre, however, is so low that the gross production of the leading crops is still below the pre-war level. The rapid progress of industrialization, the expanding needs of the population, the requirements of agricultural reconstruction and, finally, the importance of reducing the dependence of the country upon foreign sources for this class of raw materials, all dictate the necessity of energetically promoting the expansion of this division of agriculture.

Finally, a point that must be particularly emphasized is the considerable deficiency in grain production, which, if it should assume a protracted character, would become a threatening factor in the face of the growing demand of the population and the requirements of rapid industrialization. The area planted to grain in 1927-28 was 94.8 per cent of the 1913 acreage, and the total grain production in the past few years has fluctuated between 90 and 96 per cent of the average for the five years 1909 to 1913. Here is very clearly presented another crucial point in the reconstruction scheme, to which no less energy must be applied than to the metal industry. A rational solution of this problem will be secured, on the one hand, through progressive improvements in farming methods (late autumn plowing, rotation of crops, increase of live stock and of machinery, etc.) and, on the other hand, through the strengthening of the socialized sector in agriculture.

A considerable improvement has taken place, as compared with 1913, in regard to transportation conditions. The total railway mileage of the Soviet Union in 1927-28 was 30.5 per cent above that of 1913 in the same territory, and the total railway traffic was 14.4 per cent larger than in 1913.

In the course of the reconstruction period the number of workers has regained the pre-war level, real wages in industry have increased by 30 per cent as compared with 1913, and the average output per worker, by 15 per cent.

The position of the proletariat in the economic system has been strengthened.

It must be noted that these results were achieved, not only with a strict observance of the eight-hour day, but also with the taking of the initial steps in 1928-29 for the introduction of the seven-hour day.

The successful accomplishment of the currency reform in the beginning of the rehabilitation period, and the resulting stabilization, have provided the possibility of establishing the financial system on a sound basis, of organizing the budget and credit system, of mobilizing a considerable share of the national income for the financing of economic and cultural development through the medium of the government budget. In 1927-28 the combined (federal and local) budget absorbed as much as 27.5 per cent of the national income. As will be shown in a later chapter, it has been rendered possible, even before the completion of the rehabilitation period, to take up the problem of a single plan of financing for the entire economic system of the country.

The growth of the volume of production and of the productivity of labor has been reflected in an increase in the national income in 1927-28 to 107.1 per cent of the pre-war. In the five-year period ending with that year, the national income was rising at an annual rate of 10 per cent, a rate unprecedented not only in the economic history of pre-war Russia, but also in that of other incomparably more advanced countries.

Such are the main data illustrating the advance of the productive forces of the country in the reconstruction period and the economic condition of the U.S.S.R. at the outset of the five-year period covered by the present plan, as compared with pre-war Russia. Rehabilitation has been accomplished in a comparatively short time, with the country's own internal resources and without foreign aid. It has been accomplished along the lines of industrialization of the country and of the strengthening of the socialized sector of the national economy, as may be clearly seen from the following figures:

	1924-25	*1927-28*
	(Per Cent)	
(1) Share of net industrial output in total net output (including excise tax)	25.9	31.6
(2) Share of basic capital of industry in total basic capital	13.5	14.0
(3) Share of net production of the socialized sector in total national income	30.8	52.7
(4) Share of basic capital of the socialized sector in total basic capital	50.2	52.7
(5) Share of the socialized sector in total volume of trade	72.6	86.1

The five-year economic plan has been drawn up at a time when the economic development of the Soviet Union has reached a decisive turning point. Reconstruction problems of immense scope and of enormous difficulty have to be faced. The country is opening up a new page in its economic history, it is starting on a new and steep road in its development. The experience of the five-year period just elapsed has demonstrated that the Soviet Union possesses all the potentialities and all the conditions required in order to assure the broadest development of socialist economy in the near future. It is the object of the present plan to map out the program of that development for the next five years.

CHAPTER III

THE FIVE-YEAR DEVELOPMENT PROGRAM

I. GENERAL OUTLINE

THE five-year economic plan is designed to bring about a considerable advance in the process of transforming the Soviet Union from a country primarily agrarian into one predominantly industrial, both through the broad application of modern technique and through the further extension and strengthening of the principles and methods of planning a national economy. The pivotal part of the plan is the general development program.

The amount and the distribution of capital investments, the resulting changes in the structure of the national basic capital, the modifications to be brought about, as the result of the investment policy, in the comparative importance of industry and agriculture, of city and country, of socialized and private economy, and, finally, the technical methods to be applied in the construction process, these are some of the matters which must be first considered in a discussion of the plan of national economy. At the present time it is possible to present with a fair degree of precision the basic outlines of the program involving these problems and to give a concrete description of the most important construction projects.

The tremendous scope of the development program for the five years covered by the plan, and the great difficulties that will have to be overcome in realizing it, are indicated by the following table comparing the capital investments in the five-year period just elapsed and in the coming five years:

CAPITAL INVESTMENTS IN THE FIVE-YEAR PERIODS, 1923-24 TO 1927-28 AND 1928-29 TO 1932-33
(in billions of rubles, at current prices in the respective years)

	1923-24 to 1927-28	*1928-29 to 1932-33*
Total investments	26.5	64.6
Including:		
(a) Industry (including industrial housing construction)	4.4	16.4
(b) Electrification (not including industrial power plants)	0.8	3.1
(c) Transportation (including capital repairs covered by the operating budget)	2.7	10.0
(d) Agriculture	15.0	23.2
(e) Housing construction in cities (not including industrial housing)	3.6 (e and f together)	3.9
(f) Other		8.0

In the five-year period which has just elapsed the problems faced were primarily concerned with rehabilitation to the former level. Only a bare start was made in the way of a new development of the national economy. Notwithstanding the limited resources, the problems of development during that period were comparatively simple. This was especially true of new development work, which was altogether insignificant, both in

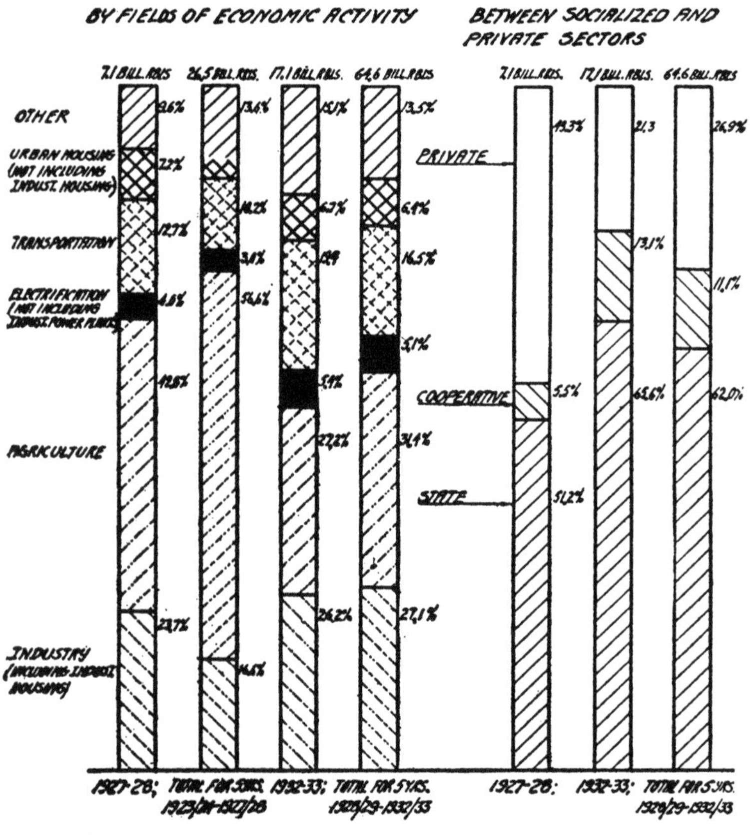

BASIC CAPITAL INVESTMENTS IN THE SOVIET UNION
(Distribution in Per Cent of Total, at Prices of Respective Years)

regard to the number of projects and their magnitude. The five-year period which is now being planned will mark the initial phase, which means the most difficult one, of new construction. The entire period will bear the impress of the new development program, conceived on a great scale, and of the formidable tasks involved in the reconstruction of old establishments, which in many cases practically means completely rebuilding and re-equipping them. By the end of the period about 35 per cent of the total industrial output is expected to come from new enterprises, not including old plants reconstructed during the period.

The experience of the past two years has demonstrated that the possibilities of expansion in the reconstruction period had been underestimated. The same experience, however, has disclosed a number of difficulties relating to organization and to technique, which had not been previously appraised at their true value, and which now have to be faced in carrying out the five-year plan of capital investments.

As the investment program is carried out, it is bound to effect a number of changes in the movement and in the structure of the basic capital of the country. These changes will fully reflect the growth of productive forces mapped out in accordance with the policy of industrialization and socialization.

The changes to be effected in the distribution of basic capital among the principal branches of national economy may be illustrated by the following figures:

BASIC CAPITAL AT THE BEGINNING AND END OF THE FIVE-YEAR PERIOD

(in billions of rubles, at 1925-26 prices)

	Oct. 1, 1928	*Oct. 1, 1933*	*Ratio of 1933 to 1928 Per Cent*
Total basic capital	70.15	127.78	182
Including:			
Industry (including housing)	9.81	29.12	297
Electrification (exclusive of power stations in industrial plants)	1.01	5.31	525
Transportation	11.65	22.01	189
Agriculture	28.74	38.89	135
Urban housing (exclusive of industrial housing)	11.97	15.25	127
Other	6.97	17.20	247

This table shows quite clearly that the growth of capital invested in industry and in electric power development will far outdistance the rate of the flow of capital into every other important field of economy.

Consequently, the relative importance of industrial capital in the distribution of the total capital will be increased to a considerable extent, as is shown by the following figures:

DISTRIBUTION OF NATIONAL CAPITAL BY PRINCIPAL DIVISIONS OF NATIONAL ECONOMY

	Oct. 1, 1928	*Oct. 1, 1933*
	Per Cent	
Industry (including industrial housing)	14.0	22.9
Electrification	1.4	4.3
Transportation	16.6	17.2
Agriculture	41.0	30.4
Housing (exclusive of industrial housing)	17.2	11.9
Other	9.8	13.3
Total	100.0	100.0

This trend of new investments will also bring about a change in the distribution of basic capital by general

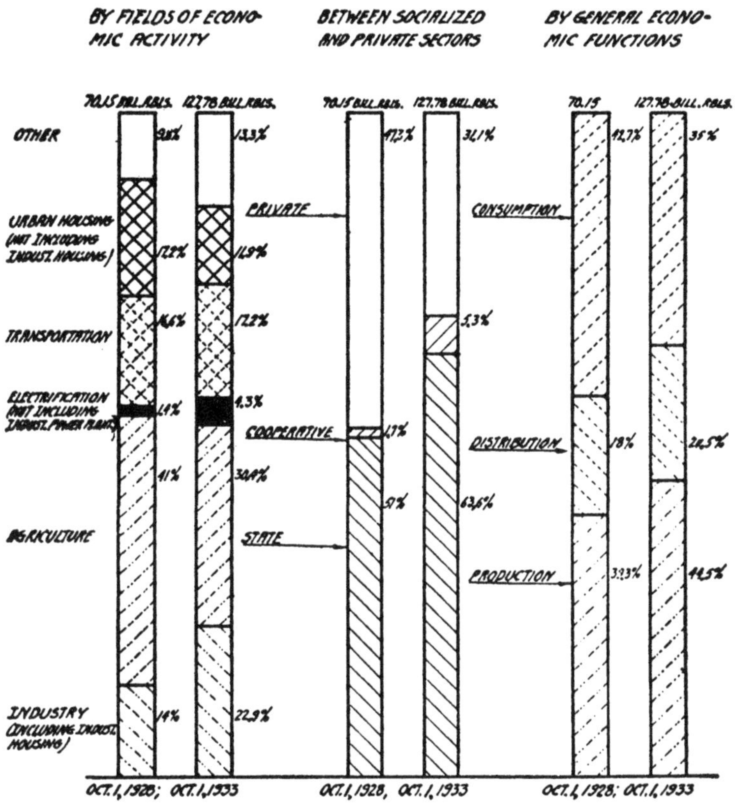

DISTRIBUTION OF BASIC CAPITAL IN THE SOVIET UNION
(Per Cent of Total)

economic functions, by increasing the relative importance of capital invested in production. This is brought out in the following table:

DISTRIBUTION OF NATIONAL CAPITAL BY GENERAL ECONOMIC FUNCTIONS

	Oct. 1, 1928	*Oct. 1, 1933*
	Per Cent	
Production	39.3	44.5
Distribution	18.0	20.5
Consumption	42.7	35.0
Total	100.0	100.0

Finally, the development program and the movement of capital will lead to a considerable strengthening of the position of the socialized sector of the national economy. The changes that will be brought about in the relative importance of the basic capital of socialized and private economy will be as follows:

DISTRIBUTION OF NATIONAL CAPITAL BETWEEN SOCIALIZED AND PRIVATE SECTORS

	Oct. 1, 1928	*Oct. 1, 1933*
	Per Cent	
State enterprises	51.0	63.6
Cooperative enterprises	1.7	5.3
Private enterprises	47.3	31.1
Total	100.0	100.0

Among the figures which indicate, in a very general manner, the characteristics of the development program for the five-year period must also be cited those showing the changes which are to be brought about in the technical level of the national economy of the Soviet Union. At the present time this phase cannot be said as yet to have been worked out in a complete or concrete manner. It is possible, however, to point out with more or less precision the factors of decisive significance in determining the technical level, namely, *the changes to be effected during the five-year period in the power situation: the kind of power generated, its consumption in various fields and the ratio of mechanical power to human labor.* These indicators deserve particular attention, especially since it is precisely in this sphere more than in any other that the Soviet Union has lagged behind the advanced industrial countries, and it is precisely here that the mightiest efforts are required in order to attain and exceed the level reached by those countries.

The fundamental change in the power situation to be effected by the program of general development will consist of a substantial increase in the importance of mechanical power in relation to the total consumption of power of all kinds, and an even more notable increase in the importance of electric power in relation to all mechanical power.

The basic figures relating to this matter will be found in the diagram and table on pages 26 and 27.

A characteristic and extremely important feature of the five-year plan, insofar as the technical phase is concerned, is the transition to large scale *enterprises combining power, chemical and metallurgical production,* embodying at once the most advanced technical achievements and the advantages of an organized and planned economy. Establishments such as the Dnieper

River power combination, the combined coke, ore and chemical works in the Donetz Basin, a similar enter-

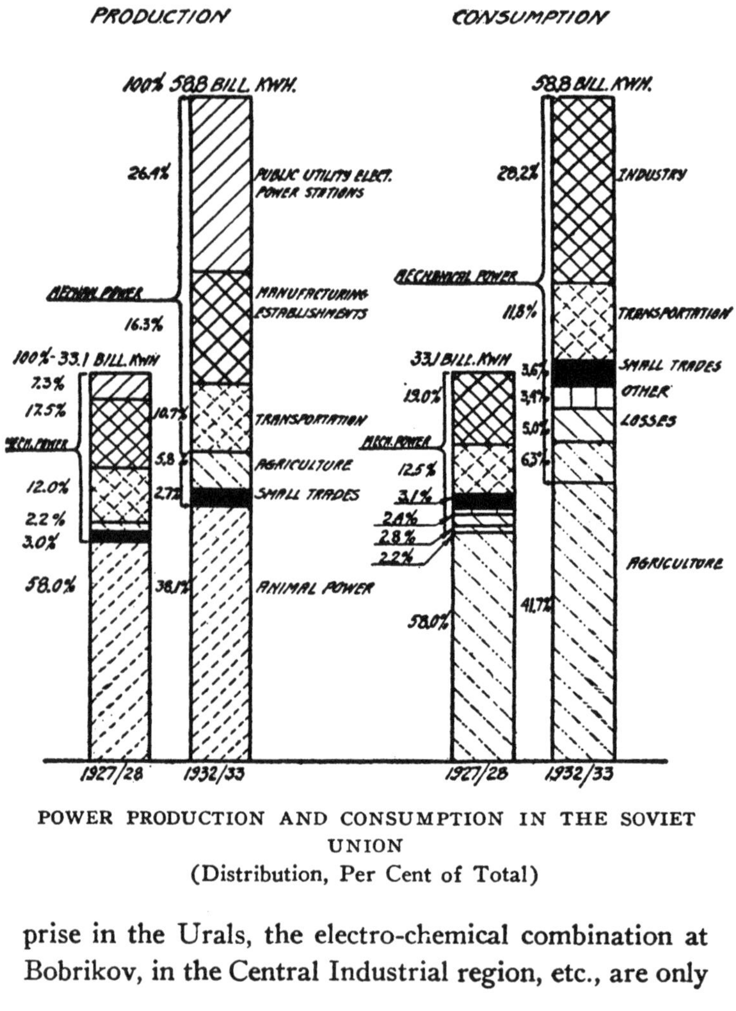

POWER PRODUCTION AND CONSUMPTION IN THE SOVIET UNION
(Distribution, Per Cent of Total)

prise in the Urals, the electro-chemical combination at Bobrikov, in the Central Industrial region, etc., are only a few of the most important milestones along the new road of technical progress on which the developing national economy of the Soviet Union is embarking.

POWER PRODUCTION

	1927-28	*1932-33*	*Ratio of 1932-33 to 1927-28 Per Cent*
Total power produced, including animal power (billions of kwh.)	33.1	58.8	177.6
Animal power utilized (billions of kwh.)	19.2	22.4	116.7
Mechanical power produced, including electric power (billions of kwh.) ..	13.9	36.4	261.9
Of which electric power produced will make up (billions of kwh.) ..	5.1	22.0	431.4
Including: Production of electric power by public utility plants, exclusive of power stations in industrial establishments (billions of kwh.)	2.4	15.5	645.8
Relative importance of mechanical power in relation to all power (per cent)	42.0	61.9	147.4
Relative importance of electric power in relation to all mechanical power (per cent)	15.4	37.4	242.8
Relative importance of electric power produced by public utility plants in relation to all mechanical power (per cent)	7.3	26.4	361.6

The above are some very general observations in regard to the five-year development program, considered as a whole. Its conformity with the general line of Soviet economic policy is obvious, as is the great scope of the development involved. The actual scale, however, of the tasks set will be clearly discerned only when the program is analyzed in its concrete applications in the principal branches of national economy.

2. ELECTRIC POWER DEVELOPMENT

The capacity of all electric power stations in the Soviet Union at the beginning of 1928-29 aggregated 1.7 million kilowatts, of which 520,000 kilowatts represented the capacity of central regional stations. The output of electric power in the fiscal year 1927-28 amounted to 5.1 billion kilowatt-hours, of which 1.9 billion kilowatt-hours was produced by central regional stations. With the economic growth of the country envisaged in the five-year plan (particularly, the sharp increase in the industrial consumption of electric power), the annual power requirements (including losses in transmission) will be, by the end of the five-year period, at least 22 billion kilowatt hours, of which 14 billion will have to be supplied by central regional power plants. According to the plan, it is the regional power plants which will have the task of solving the problem of increasing the total output of electric energy three- or four-fold, and their capacity will accordingly have to be raised from 520,000 kilowatts at the end of 1927-28 to 3,100,000 kilowatts in the last year of the period. The development program in regard to central power plants, that is, to electrification beyond purely local limits, embraces forty-two large projects. Of these, thirty-two are already under construction or being extended, while work on the remaining ten will be started during the course of the five-year period. The total length of the electric transmission systems (20,000 volts and above) will be increased from 3,000 to about 13,000 kilometers. The total amount of capital investments required in order to accomplish this expansion is estimated at 3.1 billion rubles, to which should be added another billion rubles, to be invested for power installations in individual industrial enterprises. *The amount to be invested in electric development will thus form some 24 per cent of the total investment in industry, which may be regarded as the minimum proportion if industry is to be supplied with power in accordance with modern requirements.*

It will be necessary to give here also a description of the regional aspect of this extensive and arduous program of electric power development, which is, however, the *irreducible minimum required* in order to guarantee the progress of industrialization at the rate provided under the plan. The location of the regional power plants is of special interest in its bearing upon the extremely important problem of the utilization of local fuel resources, in view of the present dependence of the principal industrial regions of the country upon mineral fuel from distant fields (Donetz Basin and Kusnetz Basin).

In the Central Industrial Region the five-year plan provides for an increase in the capacity of electric power plants from 280,000 to 1,000,000 kilowatts. Of

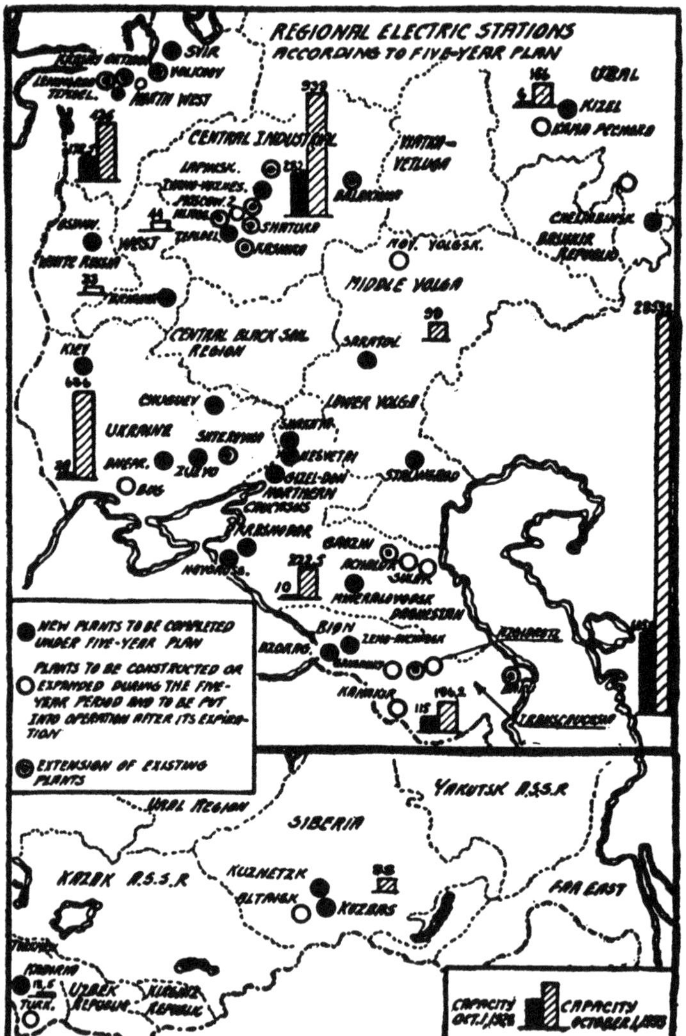
REGIONAL ELECTRIC STATIONS
ACCORDING TO FIVE-YEAR PLAN
SVIR
VOLKOV
NORTH WEST
URAL
KIZEL
CENTRAL INDUSTRIAL
SHATURA
WEST
WHITE RUSSIA
MIDDLE VOLGA
CENTRAL BLACK SOIL REGION
SARATOV
KIEV
LOWER VOLGA
UKRAINE
ZUEVO
STALINGRAD
NORTHERN CAUCASUS
DAGHESTAN
MINERALOVODSK
NEW PLANTS TO BE COMPLETED UNDER FIVE-YEAR PLAN
PLANTS TO BE CONSTRUCTED OR EXPANDED DURING THE FIVE-YEAR PERIOD AND TO BE PUT INTO OPERATION AFTER ITS EXPIRATION
EXTENSION OF EXISTING PLANTS
TRANSCAUCASIA
YAKUTSK A.S.S.R
URAL REGION
SIBERIA
KAZAK A.S.S.R
KUZNETZK
KUZBAS
FAR EAST
UZBEK REPUBLIC
KIRGHIZ REPUBLIC
TURK.
CAPACITY OCT. 1, 1928
CAPACITY OCTOBER 1, 1933

this increase, one-third will be achieved through the utilization of coal from the Moscow district, and two-thirds through the exploitation of the peat resources of the region. The outstanding projects in the development program for this region include: (a) erection of a central steam power plant in Moscow, with a capacity of 80,000 kilowatts; (b) extension of the Kashira power plant, from 12,000 to 133,000 kilowatts capacity; (c) either further extension of the Kashira plant to a capacity of 250,000 kilowatts, or construction of a new electric station at Bobrikov, with a capacity of 150,000 kilowatts; (d) extension of the Shatura plant from 92,000 to 136,000 kilowatts; (e) extension of the municipal power plants of the Moscow Province Electric Service from 100,000 to 200,000 kilowatts; (f) completion of the Ivanovo-Voznesensk station, with a capacity of 90,000 kilowatts; (g) extension of the Balakhna plant to 108,000 kilowatts, etc. In addition, work will probably be started on the construction of a second steam power plant in Moscow, further extension of the Bobrikov plant or the construction of a plant using peat at Tver, and further extension of the power stations in the Nizhni-Novgorod district.

Although the problem of the utilization of the coal of the Moscow district has been solved in a fairly satisfactory manner, neither the coal nor the peat resources of the Central Industrial Region have as yet been sufficiently investigated. Furthermore, an acute and still unsolved problem is that of reducing the cost of peat.

Work along these lines has been carried on in the past few years with great intensity and with some measure of success. The fact that the power development program for the Central Industrial Region is based entirely upon the utilization of local fuels does not mean that the dependence of the region upon the Donetz Basin will come to an end; on the contrary, as will be shown below, this dependence will be somewhat increased by the end of the five-year period.

The *Leningrad Region* now has power plants with an aggregate capacity of approximately 200,000 kilowatts. In the course of the five-year period, this capacity will be, under the plan, increased to 430,000 kilowatts. This increase will be attained through the extension of the "Krasny-Oktiabr" plant, from 20,000 to 110,000 kilowatts, of the city plants of the "Electrotok" (the company which operates the city's public utility power plants) from 84,000 to 140,000 kilowatts, and through the starting of operations in the Svir River plant, with a capacity of 80,000 kilowatts, and of the central steam power plant, with a capacity of 40,000 kilowatts. In addition, construction work will be begun on a second steam power plant in Leningrad, with a capacity of 50,000 kilowatts and on a plant on the upper Svir, or on a regional peat-utilizing plant near Malaya Vishera, with a capacity of 150,000 kilowatts. During the period Leningrad will remain one of the centers presenting difficulty in regard to power and fuel supply, and its dependence on Donetz fuel will even increase.

The Ukraine, as a whole, will be the scene of the greatest electric power development, according to the five-year plan. At the present time, the capacity of all the regional power plants in the Ukraine totals up to the small amount of 20,000 kilowatts. By the end of the five-year period the capacity of the public utility plants in the region will reach 636,000 kilowatts, including the Dnieper plant with its 330,000 kilowatts (eventual capacity 600,000 kilowatts).

The most troublesome district in regard to power supply, not only in the Ukraine, but in the entire Soviet Union, will be the Donetz Basin. At present, including power generated in industrial plants, it has an aggregate power capacity of 190,000 kilowatts. This is barely sufficient to meet the requirements of production at its present pace. It will be increased to at least 380,000 kilowatts in the five-year period through the extension of the Shterovka plant from 20,000 to 150,000 kilowatts and through an increase in the total capacity of power installations in industrial plants from 170,000 to 230,000 kilowatts. This, however, will not solve the problem of power supply for the Donetz Basin. It is essential, therefore, that upon the completion of the Dnieper River plant, it be connected by a transmission line with the Donetz Basin and that a new regional plant be built (at Zuyevo or at Toshkovo), with a capacity of 100,000 to 150,000 kilowatts.

Along with these measures, the Ukraine will complete the construction of the Kharkov plant (66,000 kilowatts) and of the Kiev plant (44,000 kilowatts).

The *Ural* region at present has a very insignificant power capacity. Inasmuch as the five-year plan assigns

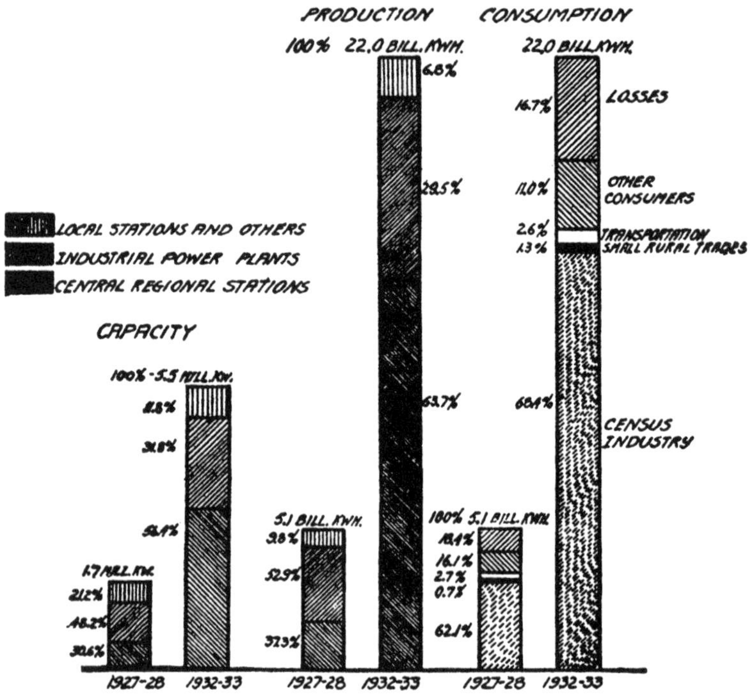

ELECTRIC POWER IN THE SOVIET UNION

to this region enormous tasks in the way of production, reconstruction and general development, the Ural will be another center where the problem of power supply will present very great difficulties. During the five-year period, the Cheliabinsk power plant (90,000 kilowatts) will be constructed and the Kiselov plant will be extended to 66,000 kilowatts. The Magnitogorsk (Magnet Mountain) Iron Works will have a power plant of high capacity, which will be inadequate, however, to serve as a central station. The fulfillment of the above program will still fall short of solving the problem of power supply in the Central Ural Region. The program, therefore, provides for starting the construction of a peat power plant in the lower Saldinsk district, where the existence of extensive peat deposits of good quality has been ascertained by prospecting, or of a plant in the Nizhni-Tagil district, to utilize blast furnace gases. The capacity of the new plant will be 50,000 kilowatts. In addition a further investigation will be made into the possibility of additional extensions to the Kiselov and Cheliabinsk plants, and the construction of a hydro-electric station with a capacity of 150,000 kilowatts at the junction of the Kama and Pechora rivers.

Northern Caucasus, where no regional power stations exist at present, is entering the five-year period with an extensive program of power development, which will give a capacity of about 200,000 kilowatts. The program includes construction of power plants at Shakhta (66,000 kilowatts), Nesvetaev (44,000 kilowatts), Baksan (25,000 kilowatts), Gisel-Don (22,000 kilowatts), Krasnodar (22,000 kilowatts) and Novorossisk (22,000 kilowatts). This great power development in a region so distinctly agrarian will undoubtedly serve to foster a considerable growth of industry here.

In the *Volga* region, the program provides for the construction of a regional power plant at Stalingrad (66,000 kilowatts) and for an extension of the Saratov plant (from 11,000 to 20,000 kilowatts). It is more than probable that this increase in power capacity will prove insufficient. But the problem of an adequate power supply for the region is bound up with that of fuel supply, which can be solved only by the realization of the Volga-Don canal project, making available to the Volga region the fuel resources of the eastern anthracite zone of the Donetz Basin. This cannot very well be accomplished within the five-year period. The plan, however, contains a tentative project for the construction of a new regional plant in the Middle Volga region, with a capacity up to 75,000 kilowatts, which may possibly utilize the shale resources of the district.

Siberia will be provided with new power capacity of 44,000 kilowatts from the Kusnetz plant and an additional 44,000 kilowatts from the Kemerovo regional plant. Both of these plants are to be considerably extended in the future.

The republics of *Central Asia* will have their power capacity increased in the aggregate by at least 50,000 kilowatts, the increase to come from a number of comparatively small plants, mainly connected with irrigation projects.

In *Transcaucasia*, the total power capacity will be at least doubled and raised to 200,000 kilowatts. This program embraces the following projects: Rion plant (extension from 21,000 to 42,000 kilowatts), Kara-Sakhal (30,000 kilowatts), Dzora (20,000 kilowatts), Kanagir (15,000 kilowatts), extension of the plant of the Azneft (Azerbaijan Oil Trust) from 85,000 to 123,000 kilowatts. In addition, in the latter part of the five-year period, it is planned to begin the construction of three regional plants in Georgia and in Azerbaijan, with an aggregate capacity of 90,000 kilowatts.

These are the general outlines, the regional aspects and the specific projects in the program of electric development, which is one of the most essential factors in furthering the industrialization of the country and strengthening its mechanical power equipment.

It must be admitted that conditions in regard to planning, research, selection of the location of plants, and the availability of a trained and reliable personnel, are far from being sufficiently favorable to guarantee the easy success of this program of electric development, especially considering the limited time within which it must be carried out. This makes the task all the more arduous and formidable and requires the concentration of tremendous efforts upon it, without the loss of a single day.

3. FUEL

The problem of electric development is closely connected with that of the fuel industries in general, and of the coal industry in particular. In order to ensure the economic development of the country in accordance with the five-year plan a steady and adequate supply of fuel, without shortages or crises, is at once one of the most important and most difficult problems to be solved. The problem must be met in such a manner as to guarantee that fuel supply shall under no conditions prove to be a limiting factor in the industrial progress of the Soviet Union, not only in the five-year period as a whole, but also—and this is of special importance—in any particular year during which the difficulties in regard to fuel supply may be exceptionally great.

To establish this fuel base of the five-year plan for national economy by utilizing only the domestic fuel resources of the Soviet Union, and at the same time to provide for the accumulation of sufficient fuel reserves, the following conditions must be met:

(a) The fuel consumption per unit of output must be reduced by at least 30 per cent in industry and 13 per cent in transportation.

(b) A broad development program for the fuel industries, and for coal in particular, must be carried out.

(c) Local fuels (local deposits of coal and, especially, peat) must be made available for the needs of the national economy.

To keep pace with the planned progress of the national economy as a whole, the increase of fuel production has been estimated as follows:

	Annual Production 1927-28	Annual Production 1932-33	Ratio of 1932-33 to 1927-28 Per Cent
1. Wood (million cubic meters) * ...	50.5	59.8	118.4
2. Peat (million tons)	6.9	16.0	231.9
3. Coal, total production (million tons)	35.4	75.0	211.9
(a) Donetz Basin	27.3	52.5	192.3
(b) Other regions	8.1	22.5	277.8
4. Crude oil, total production (million tons)	11.6	21.7	187.1
Total for all fuels (million tons of standard fuel) † ...	57.5	104.8	182.3

* For industrial requirements only, exclusive of consumption of urban population and government offices.
† This total has been obtained by adding the quantities of the several fuels, in standard fuel equivalents. One kilogram of "standard fuel" is equivalent to 7,000 calories.

The industrial consumption of the various fuels in 1927-28 and 1932-33 and their relative weight in the total industrial consumption are as follows:

	1927-28 Industrial Consumption	Per Cent of Total Industrial Consumption, in Standard Fuel Equivalent	1932-33 Industrial Consumption	Per Cent of Total Industrial Consumption, in Standard Fuel Equivalent
1. Wood (millions of cubic meters)	50.34	17.6	58.5	11.4
2. Peat (millions of tons)	5.53	4.8	14.4	7.1
3. Total coal (millions of tons)	34.43	59.4	68.6	65.3
Donetz Basin coal	26.88	48.4	48.4	49.2
Other coal	7.55	11.0	20.2	16.1
4. Oil fuels (millions of tons)	6.86	18.2	10.8	16.2
Total (millions of "standard fuel" tons)	53.82	100.0	95.4	100.0

It can be seen from the above that the relative importance of wood and oil in the total fuel consumption will diminish, that of peat will be somewhat augmented, while that of coal will increase considerably. It is interesting to note that the relative importance of Donetz fuel will also increase, notwithstanding the large expansion of the coal production of other fields. In other words, all during the five-year period the Central Industrial Region and the Leningrad Region, as well as the Ural Region, will be increasingly dependent upon coal from distant fields, namely, from the Donetz Basin in the first two cases and from the Kusnetz Basin for the Urals.

The COAL production quotas assigned to the various districts at the end of the five-year period, as compared with last year, are as follows:

	1927-28		*1932-33*	
	Production, in Millions of Tons	*Per Cent of Total Production*	*Production, in Millions of Tons*	*Per Cent of Total Production*
1. Donetz Basin ..	27.26	77.0	52.5	70.1
2. Kusnetz Basin..	2.46	7.0	6.0	8.0
3. Urals	2.00	5.6	6.1	8.1
4. Moscow district	1.18	3.3	4.2	5.6
5. Eastern Siberia.	1.91	5.4	4.0	5.3
6. Central Asia ...	0.23	0.7	1.0	1.3
7. Caucasus	0.11	0.3	0.6	0.8
8. All other	0.25	0.7	0.6	0.8
Total	35.40	100.0	75.0	100.0

These production totals to be attained in the different fields will determine the distribution of capital investments provided for the coal industry under the plan. The total amount to be invested in the coal industry as a whole during the five years is about 1,250 million rubles, of which about three-fourths will go to the Donetz Basin.

The *Donetz Basin* faces the tremendous task of increasing its coal output from 27 million tons in 1927-28 to 52.5 million tons in 1932-33. This means increasing its production capacity to 55 million tons a year. The mines now in operation, together with the 17 new mines on which construction has begun, will assure by the end of the five-year period a total producing capacity of about 41 million tons. It is estimated that the development of large mines requires from 3½ to 5 years, of medium-size mines from 2 to 3 years, while the reconstruction and extension of old mines of considerable capacity takes from 1½ to 3 years. From this it follows that, in order to secure the necessary fuel supply during the planned period and to accomplish the requisite preparatory work for the needs of the succeeding five-year period, the following tasks must be carried out:

(a) The work that has been started on the thirteen new large mines and on the four mines being reconstructed must be rushed to completion at an accelerated pace;

(b) About forty old large mines must be radically reconstructed and extended;

(c) Beginning with 1929-30, construction must be

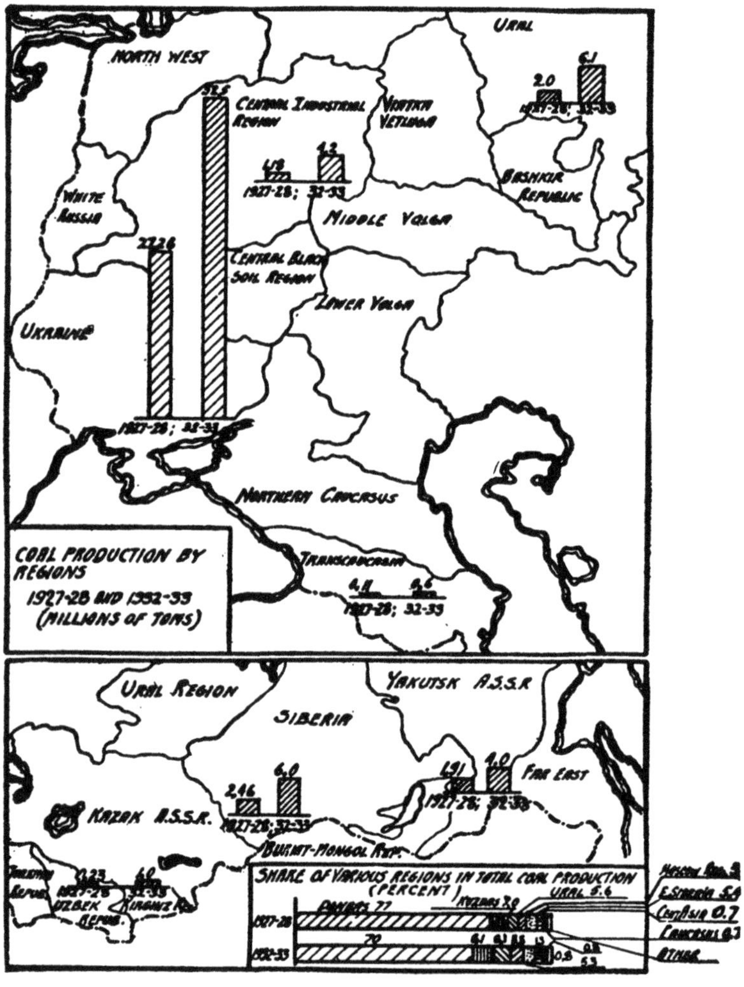

COAL PRODUCTION IN THE SOVIET UNION

begun on a series of new large mines, at the annual rate of 10 to 12 units with an aggregate capacity of 6.5 million tons a year, so that by the end of the period there will be about 50 new large mines at various stages of construction and equipment;

(d) Complete mechanization of all new mines must be effected, and also, to a considerable extent, that of the reconstructed mines, so that by the end of the five-year period not less than 70 to 75 per cent of the coal output of the Donetz Basin will be mined with machinery;

(e) The problem of an adequate water supply for the Donetz Basin must be solved;

(f) Likewise, the electrification requirements of the region must be satisfied;

(g) An extensive program of housing construction must be carried out, involving a capital outlay of from 240 to 260 million rubles;

(h) Prospecting must be carried on at an intensified pace.

To carry out the development program for the coal industry of the Donetz Basin, capital investments of 800 to 850 million rubles will be required. Neither the formidable size of the program, nor the tremendous difficulties to be overcome should be underestimated. It is sufficient to state that the program lacks the assurance that might be afforded by reliable prospecting surveys, that there are at the present time hardly any detailed plans prepared for the proposed series of new mines, and that the technical personnel available in the Donetz Basin is as yet insufficient to carry out the program with strict observance of the time limits, which is essential if the fuel supply of the country is to show the required growth. The program, however, is the strict minimum required in order to insure the industrial development of the country embodied in the five-year plan.

From the standpoint of the general economic development of the Soviet Union, the *Ural region* and the *Kusnetz Basin* must be considered as a single unit in regard to fuel production. The production quotas of these districts involve increasing the coal output of the Ural region from 2 million tons in 1927-28 to 6.1 million tons in 1932-33, and of the Kusnetz Basin from 2.5 million to 6.0 million tons. While this production plan may appear insignificant in absolute amount, the development program which it necessitates is proportionately not any easier—but undoubtedly even more difficult—of attainment than that assigned to the Donetz Basin coal industry. In the Urals it will be necessary to begin construction work on about twenty mines, including eight large ones, and to carry it through to completion during the period. In the Kusnetz Basin six mines will have to be re-equipped and eight new large mines will have to be started, two of which will be of a larger capacity (up to a million tons annually each) than has hitherto been known in either of these two districts. The capital outlays required will be about 100 million rubles for the Urals and 75 million rubles for the Kusnetz Basin.

The difficulties in the way of carrying out this program in the Ural region and in the Kusnetz Basin arise from the general technical unpreparedness of the two districts for development work on so large a scale, and from the extremely inadequate prospecting thus far accomplished. The planning work for new construction projects is even less advanced here than in the Donetz Basin. However, even this program is obviously insufficient, especially insofar as the Kusnetz Basin with its enormous coal reserves is concerned. For this reason it is absolutely necessary to re-examine the question of more effectively uncovering these reserves and making them available for the national economy.

The *Moscow district* will have to increase its coal output from 1.2 million tons in 1927-28 to 4.2 million tons in 1932-33. This will require the opening of from four to six large mines, of an annual capacity of 350,-000 to 650,000 tons each, a radical departure from the small mines now existing in the district, still operated to a great extent by semi-primitive methods. The capital to be invested in the five-year period is estimated at about 45 million rubles. The program for this district, as in the case of the Kusnetz Basin, cannot be regarded as adequate, and additional investigations must be made into the possibility of further expansion.

The remaining coal districts, including the Far East,

Cheremkhov, Central Asia, Tkvarcheli, etc., are also assigned comparatively big production tasks, involving aggregate investments of about 60 million rubles.

The development program for the PETROLEUM INDUSTRY is based upon considerations of much more complicated character than the requirements of fuel supply, which here play only a subordinate part. The plan provides for an increase in the oil output from 11.6 million tons in 1927-28 to 21.7 million tons in 1932-33. However, when the planned rate of growth of oil production is compared with the rate of growth in the other leading oil-producing countries, the attainments aimed at under the plan must be regarded as insufficient. New possibilities for further expansion of oil production must, therefore, be sought, through more extensive prospecting in new districts and more intensive new construction work.

Along with this, another, and no less important, object of the petroleum development program is the more than doubling of the capacity of oil refineries—from 8.7 million tons in 1927-28 to 19.1 million tons in 1932-33. In addition, extensive use of cracking for the treatment of fuel oil will be introduced during the five-year period; it is planned to have 55 cracking plants installed in 1932-33. Finally, the plan provides, besides the completion of the pipe-lines under way, for the construction of two additional pipe-lines. In the event of favorable results of the prospecting work in the Emba field, work will be started before the expiration of the period on the construction of a refinery in Samara and, probably, a pipe-line from Emba to Samara (about 600 kilometers).

The realization of this development program for the oil industry will bring about such a rate of growth

FIVE-YEAR PLAN FOR THE PETROLEUM INDUSTRY

	1927-28	*1932-33*	*Ratio of 1932-33 to 1927-28 Per Cent*
1. Production of crude oil (millions of tons):			
(a) Petroleum	11.3	20.8	184.1
(b) Natural gas	0.3	0.9	300.0
Total	11.6	21.7	187.1
2. Refining operations (millions of tons):			
(a) Crude petroleum	8.7	19.1	219.5
(b) Fuel oils	1.7	8.4	494.1
3. Consumed by oil industry and lost in refining (millions of tons)	1.8	3.3	183.3
4. Commercial output by main producing groups (millions of tons):			
(a) Motor fuels (for automobile, airplane, tractor and other motors)	1.8	6.1	338.9
(b) Refined products other than fuel (illuminating oils, lubricants, etc.)	2.7	4.8	177.8
(c) Fuel oil.............	5.4	7.5	138.9
Total commercial output (millions of tons)	9.9	18.4	185.9
Value of commercial output (millions of rubles)	275.0	645.3	234.7
Average cost per ton (rubles)	27.8	35.1	126.3

in oil production and refining and such a relationship between them as will mean further substantial progress in the rationalization of this extremely important branch of Soviet industry.

The foregoing table requires little comment. It shows that the planned progress in the refining of crude oil and, especially, of fuel oil (by the cracking process), will outstrip the growth in crude production, decreasing the relative importance of oil as a fuel.

The total amount of capital to be invested in the petroleum industry during the five-year period has been figured at 1.4 billion rubles. In regard to the special difficulties in the way of this program of development and production it need only be mentioned that up to 4.5 million tons of the annual crude production provided under the plan is to come from fields on which prospecting has not as yet been completed. This necessitates the carrying out of the program of prospecting in the oil industry with the utmost speed and energy.

The production of PEAT, as has been shown above, will have to be increased nearly two and a half times. This cannot be regarded as sufficient, from the point of view of increasing the relative importance of local fuels. However, a further extension of the program of peat production will depend on a solution of the problem of widening the market for peat products (briquetting, distillation, etc.).

The five-year plan for the peat industry will require a capital investment of about 195 million rubles.

The scope of the development program in fuel production demands that the greatest attention be concentrated upon this sector of the construction front. In view of what has been outlined above in regard to the development of electrification and fuel production and the changes in the general fuel and power economy—considering the close interdependence between these matters and the problems of power in industry, transportation, municipal enterprises and, eventually, agriculture also—one inescapable conclusion stands out, namely, that the organizations connected with power problems should be greatly strengthened and their work coordinated in a single power center. The creation of an efficient central power board is a matter that requires urgent and immediate action.

4. METAL INDUSTRY AND MACHINE CONSTRUCTION

The attainment of the goals set in relation to power and fuel, as described above, will clear the way for the accomplishment of one of the most important and formidable tasks embodied in the five-year plan, namely, the accelerated development of the metal and machine industries in the Soviet Union.

It is not a casual circumstance that the degree of industrial progress of a country is measured, in the first instance, by the condition of its metal and machine industries. Likewise, it is not by accident that in plans for the economic development of the Soviet Union, the metal problems are given the greatest attention. In the five-year period covered by the present plan the metal and the machine industries will be the most important link in the construction program, and on them the greatest resources and the most strenuous efforts will be concentrated.

Of all the capital investments in industry, which will total 16.4 billion rubles in the five years, *4 billions will go into the metal and machine industry, the largest investment provided for any single industry, not excluding electrification.* This investment program is based upon preliminary estimates of the iron requirements of the country, which are figured at 9.8 million tons for 1932-33, as compared with about 4 million tons in 1928-29. These estimates, though conditional and subject to such modifications as may be dictated by actual developments, may, nevertheless, be regarded as sufficiently reliable for practical purposes. The requirements of pig iron for the five-year period as a whole are figured at 32.7 million tons, of rolled steel—31.5 million, rails—3.2 million, bars—14.1 million, sheet iron—4.2 million, roofing-iron—3.1 million, etc. In order to satisfy the requirements of pig iron 100 per cent, and of other varieties of iron to the extent of 80 or 95 per cent, it is necessary to provide for a minimum annual output of 10 million tons of metal in 1932-33, or nearly three times the output of 1927-28.

The development program for the iron and steel industry has been drawn up in accordance with these considerations. It is to be carried out, on the one hand, through the extensive reconstruction of the metal works now in operation in the two main metal producing centers (the Ukraine and the Urals) and, on the other hand, through the construction of a number of new plants, both in the old centers and in new districts, namely, the Kerch Peninsula and the Kusnetz Basin.

The post-war experience of Germany, which has been followed with interest by all advanced industrial countries, has demonstrated that the productivity of steel plants may be considerably increased, if more thorough attention is given to the work in the preparatory stages (ore concentration, proper selection of coke, better preparation of the furnace charge in general). The application of these methods, the value of which has been sufficiently proven, and the proper reconstruction of the existing metal works, will make it possible to increase their output to 7.4 million tons, with the Ukraine increasing its output from 2.4 million tons in 1927-28 to at least 5.6 million tons in 1932-33, the Urals—from 0.7 millions to 1.4 millions, etc. This increase in the output of existing metal works will require the *construction of 12 to 15 new blast furnaces in the Ukraine during the five-year period,* with a capacity of 180,000 to 200,000 tons a year each (not including furnaces to be rebuilt) and a general reconstruction of the plants corresponding to the extension of the furnace capacity. As a result, the *average annual production capacity per blast furnace in the South-*

ern district will increase from 85,000 tons in the current year to 125,000 tons in 1932-33. In the Urals the problem involves the construction at existing plants of *about 10 blast furnaces* (using mineral fuel), with an average annual capacity of 180,000 tons; the feeding in the large units will be completely mechanized, a type of furnace hitherto entirely unknown in the metal industry of the Urals.

The reconstruction of the existing metal works (including the necessary expansion of ore mining and the organization of coke production, which is also one of the most complex problems of the five-year period) will require a capital investment of approximately one billion rubles. Of this, about three-fourths will go to the Southern district and one-fourth to the Urals. *A special difficulty of the plan is the fact that the reconstruction of the existing works will have to be carried on in the face of an acute shortage of iron and steel, and it will, therefore, be impossible to suspend work at the plants for any considerable length of time.* For this reason the plan of reconstruction will have to be worked out with the greatest care and carried out under organized systematic guidance. It goes without saying that provisions will have to be made to secure an adequate and uninterrupted delivery of supplies and of imported equipment, as well as technical assistance by foreign experts. Inasmuch as the entire program of metal production in the five years hinges on this reconstruction, it must be conducted with the closest cooperation of all concerned and under the strictest control.

Whereas the country's metal supply during the five-year period covered by the plan will be obtained through the reconstruction of existing metal works, *the construction of new plants, which is now being started on a tremendous scale, will satisfy the additional metal requirements in the last year of the period and, especially, all through the succeeding five-year period.* It is the task of the five-year period covered by the present plan partly to start and partly to prepare for the starting of that new series of gigantic metal plants, the presence of which alone will make it possible to advance with requisite speed on this decisive front in the industrialization of the country. That is why the plan provides for investments in the construction of new metal works nearly equal in amount (almost one billion rubles) to the capital outlay provided for the reconstruction of existing plants.

In the last year of the five-year period the new metal works will have an aggregate output of 2.6 million tons of pig iron. This will come not only from the two old metal-producing districts (the Ukraine and the Urals) but also from the Kerch district and from the Kusnetz Basin. The plan for new construction adopts as the standard type a large plant of annual capacity of 650,000 tons, with provision for further subsequent expansion, up to double that capacity, wherever conditions in regard to location and raw materials are favorable for such development. As regards the distribution of the new plants, the plan is dictated by the necessity of having them adjoin the sources of raw materials and power supply, although it also permits of such extended industrial combinations as those of the Urals and Kusnetz districts, Kerch-Tkvarcheli and Zaporozhie-Krivoy Rog.

The following specific new construction projects in the iron industry may be regarded as definitely adopted for the five-year period:

(a) *Kerch group,* with a total capacity of 750,000 tons, at a cost of about 150 million rubles.

(b) *Ukrainian group,* including a plant at Krivoy-Rog with a capacity of 650,000 tons; one at Zaporozhie, with a similar capacity; the Dnieprosplav plant (100,000 tons); the Electric Steel Works at Dniepropetrovsk; and the Mariupol plant. The total cost of this group is about 350 million rubles. In addition, the question will have to be investigated as to the advisability of constructing a metal plant in the Donetz Basin or of doubling the capacity of one of the other Ukrainian plants (Krivoy-Rog or Zaporozhie), which will also require 100 to 150 million rubles.

(c) *The Ural group,* including the Magnitogorsk metal works, with an annual capacity of 650,000 tons, the Alapayevsk plant, the Zlatoust special steel plant and the Balashov plant, with an aggregate cost of about 210 million rubles for the four plants; the Tavdinsk

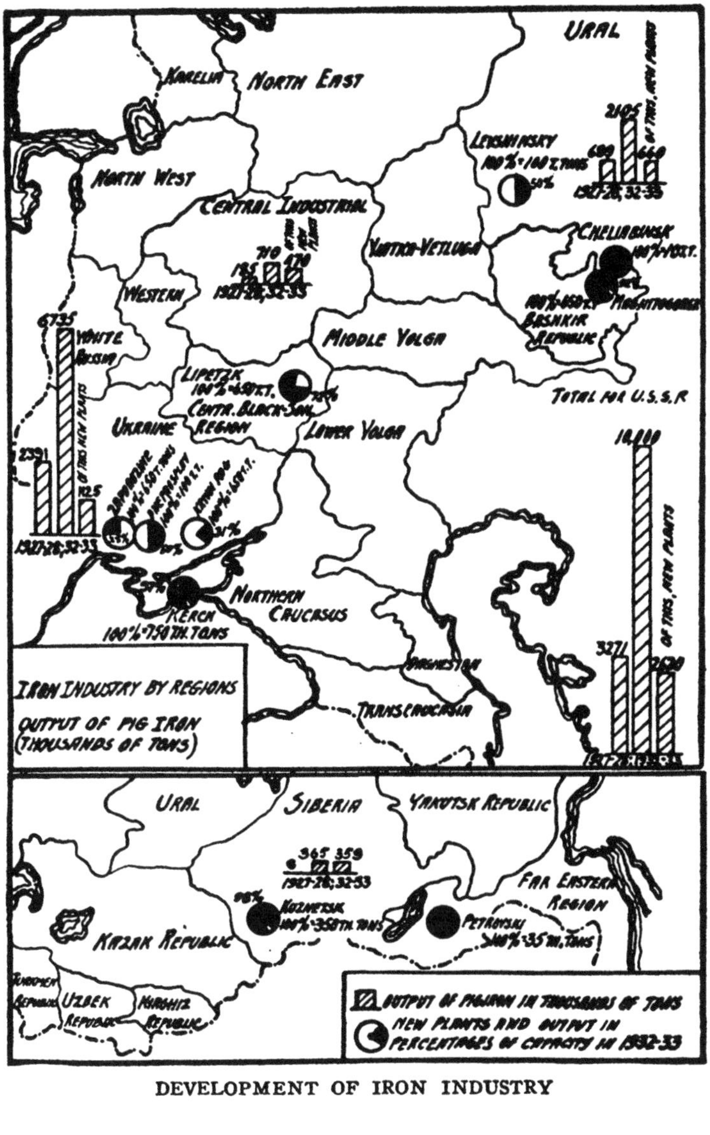

DEVELOPMENT OF IRON INDUSTRY

works with an annual production capacity of 50,000 tons of pig iron, the Cheliabinsk ferro-steel plant, the Saldinsk and the Nadejdinsk sheet iron works, and a number of smaller plants, at an aggregate cost of about 75 million rubles; in addition, the Kama and the Kamenka plants with a capacity of 50,000 tons each.

(d) *The Siberian group,* consisting of the Kusnetz (Telbes) plant, with an annual capacity of 350,000 tons, at a cost of about 130 million rubles, and the Far Eastern plant at Petrovsk, with a capacity of 30,000 tons, at a cost of at least 12 million rubles.

(e) Finally, the following projects are under consideration: (1) in the Central Industrial Region, the Lipetzk plant, with a capacity of 650,000 tons, at a cost of about 180 million rubles; (2) in the Central Black Soil Region, Khopersk plant, with a capacity of 650,000 tons, at a cost of about 180 million rubles, and (3) in the Caucasus, a metallurgical plant at a cost of about 100 million rubles, and the organization of the production of ferro-manganese for export, with the utilization of electric power from the Rion and the Daghestan power plants. It is quite possible that instead of these projects it will be found more expedient to provide a considerably enlarged capacity of some of the new metal works constructed in other districts, where the supply of both raw materials and power is better secured.

This new development work in the metal industry is the foundation of the vast program of machine construction. Through the building of new coking plants and blast furnaces it also, as will be seen below, affords a basis for the accelerated growth of the chemical industry, which is, in turn, a prerequisite for the reorganization of agriculture and for the increase of the defensive power of the country. The metal industry is thus one of the most vital branches in the country's economic development, and also one of the most difficult—especially since the existing conditions require that the development projects be completed within the shortest possible time (in not more than four or five building seasons). At the present time, however, out of the array of metal works enumerated above, detailed plans have been drawn only for the plants at Magnitogorsk, Kusnetz and Krivoy-Rog. The most strenuous efforts directed toward the early completion of plans, specifications, surveys, etc., are essential for success in this field.

The object of the program of investments in the iron and steel industry is, of course, not only to secure a large output, but also *to bring a considerable improvement in the quality of the product and to lower the cost of production.* The average production cost of pig iron in the Ural plants is estimated at 46.7 rubles a ton by the end of the five-year period, as compared with 55.9 rubles at the beginning, and in the Ukraine plants, 38.2 rubles as compared with 49.9 rubles.

The difficulties to be expected in the non-ferrous industries are of no lesser magnitude. The projected growth of the production of non-ferrous metals during the five-year period is shown in the following table (including concession enterprises):

	1927-28	*1932-33*
	(thousands of metric tons)	
Copper	28.3	85.0
Zinc	3.25	77.0
Lead	3.02	38.5
Aluminum	....	5.0

The realization of this production program, which must be regarded as a minimum when the tempo of the general reconstruction process is considered, is conditioned upon the carrying out of development work of great scope and complexity, involving capital outlays of about 450 million rubles for the period.

The *machine construction industry* of the Soviet Union has achieved considerable progress and has been rising high above the insignificant position it occupied in Russia prior to the war. However, all that has been so far accomplished is only a faint start on the road to a solution of the formidable problems of the industry, which, to a great extent, will have to be solved within the period embraced by the plan. It is in this field that the way lies toward raising the productivity of labor in all branches of national economy to higher levels. That is why the five-year plan includes, besides the capital investments in the iron and steel and non-ferrous metal industries, a provision for the investment of about one billion rubles for capital construction in the machine-building industries.

The specific projects involved in this program are determined primarily by the existing conditions in regard to available mechanical power and by the problems arising from these conditions. According to the most conservative estimates, nearly one-half of the *boiler* resources of Soviet industry, i.e., about 800,000 square meters of heating surface, is at the present time both obsolete and deteriorated. In addition, about one-half of all motors in industry, i.e., about 700,000 horse-power, are obsolete and partly deteriorated. To this should be added the new demand for mechanical equipment arising from the general economic progress of the country. These circumstances dictate the necessity of building up the boiler construction industry and of raising it to a new technical level. The Metal Works in Leningrad, the Parostroy in Moscow, and the boiler plant at Taganrog specialize along these lines, and together they will account, by the end of the five-year period, for about 70 per cent of the total production of boilers, which will increase from 114,000 square meters of heating surface in 1927-28 to 300,000 square meters in 1932-33. The construction of *Diesel engines* will be concentrated chiefly at the Kolomna plant, the "Russky Diesel," in Leningrad, and at the Sormovo plant; about 70 per cent of the total production of Diesel engines, which will rise during the period from 65,900 hp. to 202,000 hp., will come from these plants. *Turbine* construction is centered mainly at the Leningrad Metal Works, which will increase its output in the course of the five-year period from 60,000 kw. in capacity to 650,000 kw. Hydraulic turbines are also included in the production schedule of one of the plants of the Moscow Machine Trust.

In the same group may be included, to a certain extent, the growth of *machine-tool* production. This will be attained primarily through enlarging the present centers of production (the Sverdlov plant in Leningrad, "Krasny Proletary" in Moscow, "Dvigatel Revolutsii" in Nizhni-Novgorod, and the Kramator plant), through the reorganization of a number of smaller plants and the erection of new plants in the Ukraine, the Central Region, and possibly, in the Ural region. The development of machine-tool construction in the U.S.S.R. requires during the five-year period an investment of 25,000,000 rubles for new plants only.

Another important consideration which determines the machine building program is the need of highly specialized *equipment for the principal mining districts* in the Soviet Union,—in the southern district, the Urals and Siberia. To meet these requirements, the program provides for a complete rebuilding of the Kramator machine plant, which involves investments of about 45,000,000 rubles, and the completion of the heavy machine construction plant at Sverdlovsk, in the Ural region, at a total cost of about 49,000,000 rubles. The completion of these projects will result in a proper distribution of the basic *centers of heavy machine construction throughout the country;* the disadvantages of long hauls will be done away with, and the reorganization of mining, which is essential in order to secure the increase in the production of coal, iron ore, non-ferrous metals, etc., demanded by the general plan of economic development, will be assured.

The next factor of importance in the program of machine construction in the five-year period is transportation and the problems of its further development. In the succeeding pages a detailed description will be given of the program for the upbuilding of the transportation system and the demands upon the metal industry for locomotives, cars, automatic couplings, etc., which this work will involve. In accordance with this program, provisions have been made for reconstruction of existing *locomotive works,* which will require a total investment of up to 100,000,000 rubles in the half-decade. The principal reconstruction project will be the Lugansk plant, in which about 40,000,000 rubles will be invested and which is scheduled to increase its output to 350 high-powered locomotives by 1932-33. Only toward the end of the period will the question of the reconstruction on a large scale of another locomotive plant (either that of Sormovo or of Kharkov) be taken up; this will have to be postponed until an additional study of the problem has been completed. The development of *car-building* will be carried out chiefly through the reorganization of existing plants, which is now under way. There will be added, however, the car-building division of the Dneprovsk plant, which will be completely rebuilt, and a new car-building plant at Nizhni-Tagil in the Urals. The two latter plants will become the principal centers of the construction of heavy freight cars. The total investment required for the car-building plants is estimated at 160,000,000 rubles. In order to prepare for the introduction of automatic coupling of railway cars, *one or two plants will have to be constructed, at a total cost of from 30,000,000 to 50,000,000 rubles.* In all probability, the plants will be located in the Ukraine and in the Ural district.

Finally, as also a part of the machine construction program to meet transportation needs, there should be mentioned the *shipbuilding* program, both for maritime and river vessels, for which a capital outlay of 82,000,000 rubles has been provided.

Especial attention must be paid to the problem of developing *automobile* production. The plan provides for the construction of an automobile plant at Nizhni-Novgorod, at a cost of 140,000,000 rubles, which will have an annual output of 100,000 cars. This is a decisive step towards a solution of this extremely important economic and cultural problem.

In regard to the branch of the metal industry which supplies various materials and equipment for the building trades, in particular, *the production of construction machinery,* which is just beginning to develop in the Soviet Union, provision is made for a plant to produce such machinery, to be erected in the Central Industrial Region at a cost of about 12,000,000 rubles.

The factories which will produce textile machinery, chemical equipment, etc., though involving a small capital outlay, are of prime importance as pioneers in their respective fields.

Finally, there is a tremendous task in regard to the production of *agricultural machinery*. This is directly linked up with the problem of agricultural reconstruction, the solution of which is one of the most essential prerequisites for the success of the entire economic plan. The program in regard to the manufacture of agricultural machinery is designed to bring the value of the annual output up to 610,000,000 rubles by the end of the five-year period, as against 153,000,000 rubles in 1927-28. That goal will be reached through the completion of the Rostov plant, at a cost of 46,000,000 rubles, extensive reconstruction of the Ukrainian plants, which will require a capital investment of 58.6 million rubles, rebuilding of a number of plants in the Russian Republic proper, with an outlay of 30.3 million rubles, and erection of an agricultural machinery plant at Omsk. The total amount to be invested in the production of agricultural machinery has been estimated at 180,000,000 rubles.

The most weighty tasks in this field are concerned with the development of *tractor* production. These involve the *construction of the Stalingrad tractor plant,* at a cost of 77,000,000 rubles and with an annual output of 50,000 tractors, the enlargement of the tractor department of the Putilov works, in Leningrad, in order to increase its output to 20,000 units a year, and of the tractor department of the Kharkov locomotive works, to attain an annual output of 3,000 tractors. Furthermore, it has been decided to begin the construction in 1929-30 of another large tractor plant in the Urals, to have a capacity similar to that of the Stalingrad plant.

Such are the general outlines and the principal objects of the development program for the machine construction industry. This description covers, of course, only the most essential points of the vast, complex and many-sided program. The general tendency will be to confine the assortment of machinery to as few types as possible and to meet the new machine building problems gradually, as they arise, thus assuring an accumulation of experience and securing every foothold gained before proceeding further. Nevertheless, the requirements of national industrialization insistently dictate the constant introduction of new groups of machinery plants, many of which will attain only the initial stage of development in the course of the five-year period.

The expansion of the machine construction industry is distributed over nearly all the principal industrial regions, and the apportionment of capital as between rebuilding and new construction has been made in a manner that apparently responds to the needs of a rational development of the productive forces of the country.

It is unnecessary to stress the enormous importance of the development program in the metal and machine industry. *It is the pivot on which the entire plan of economic construction hinges.* But it is extremely important to emphasize the tremendous difficulties and, consequently, the tremendous responsibilities involved in this phase of the construction work, which is the first in importance and in the amounts of investments required, and which will not only heavily tax the resources and the organizing talent of the country, but will also necessitate considerable technical aid from the advanced countries of Europe and from America.

5. CHEMICAL INDUSTRY

One of the tasks to be accomplished in the five-year period is the *creation of a new industry in the Soviet Union—the chemical industry.* Its tremendous importance for nearly all other branches of industry, for agricultural reconstruction, for the rationalization of forestry, and for the general cultural development of the country, cannot be overstated. Whether through the utilization of waste substances, the application of chemical methods for the most efficient use of raw materials, the creation of power consuming processes, or through the absorption of waste of power plants, the work of the chemical industry is intimately interwoven with a number of other industries and is one of the most important factors in the development of the country's economic system as a whole.

The scope of the development program in the chemical industry is determined by the production goals to be attained in the five-year period. The output of acid phosphate fertilizers (figured in the equivalent of standard superphosphate) will have to be increased from 150,000 tons in 1927-28 to 3.4 million tons in 1932-33. As the operations of the Kerch steel mill develop, the deliveries of Thomas slag will be gradually increasing, until they reach 85,000 tons (in equivalent of standard 14 per cent superphosphate) at the end of the period. The output of ground phosphorite, which now amounts to 65,000 tons a year, will be increased to 1.2 million tons, while that of nitrogen fertilizers (figured in equivalents of ammonium sulphate) will be increased from 5,000 to 800,000 tons. The production of potassium salts—an industry entirely new for the Soviet Union—is planned to attain a total of 1.5 million tons by the end of the five-year period. The total output of chemical fertilizers should reach 7.2 million tons by 1932-33.

This production program, which must be carried out in full if failure is to be prevented in the most important branches of the general economic plan, agriculture, etc., is conditioned entirely upon the completion of extensive development work, which involves *a capital investment of 1.4 billion rubles in the chemical industry,* whereas the entire capital now invested in the industry amounts to about 400 million rubles.

The importance of the chemical industry as a consumer of power and as a utilizer of the waste products of power plants links its development with the plan of power development outlined above. Accordingly, the construction of chemical plants will be concentrated chiefly in the following districts: (a) Donetz Basin; (b) the territory adjoining the Dnieprostroy power plant; (c) the Central Industrial Region with its coal and peat resources; (d) the Urals, where the by-products of coal combustion, coking, and non-ferrous metal smelting will be utilized; (e) the North West Region, with its peat deposits, lumber industry, and hydroelectric resources; and, partly, (f) the Kusnetz Basin, Central Asia and Transcaucasia.

The *Ukraine,* or, more specifically, its mining section (Donetz Basin, the Dnieprostroy and Krivoy-Rog districts), is called upon to achieve the greatest results in the five-year period in regard to chemical development and to become a powerful center of the chemical industry. The program provides for the construction and starting of synthetic ammonia plants, some to be connected with coking establishments, and for the installation of equipment for converting fixed nitrogen into mineral fertilizers. The soda plant now in operation will be greatly enlarged, and its annual capacity will be brought up to 300,000 tons of calcined soda. In addition, a new soda plant with a capacity of up to 200,000 tons will be constructed. In the Dnieprostroy district the construction of a large chemical plant is on the program. The total amount of capital to be invested in the chemical industry of the Ukraine is estimated at about 350,000,000 rubles.

In the *Central Industrial Region* a large fertilizer establishment will be created, at a total cost of about 50,000,000 rubles, with an annual capacity of 250,000 tons of sulphuric acid and 400,000 tons of acid phosphates. The operation of this plant will be based on the Egoriev phosphate deposits and the Bobrikov power combine. The special field, however, assigned to the Central Industrial Region is not the production of basic chemicals, but that of refined chemical products, such as dyes, pharmaceuticals, rubber products, rare elements, etc. The establishment of a large chemical enterprise near Moscow will pave the way to a solution of the problem of artificial silk production. Finally, the peat-using electric station in the Yaroslavl district will be utilized for a large rubber plant, designed to meet the growing demand for automobile tires, inner tubes, etc. A total of about 240,000,000 rubles will be invested in the chemical industry in this region.

The *North West Region,* or, more specifically, the city of Leningrad, affords the most suitable location for superphosphate production, with the use of imported phosphorites. For this purpose it is intended to construct here a new plant, with a capacity of 200,000 tons of superphosphates, which will eventually work with raw materials from domestic sources, namely, from the newly discovered high content acid phosphate deposits in the Murmansk Railroad region (the Khibinsk deposits). Besides, the construction of an artificial silk factory is already under way in Leningrad, and in this connection the production of a number of chemicals (caustic soda, carbon bisulphide, etc.) will have to be organized. The total to be invested in the North West Region is estimated at about 80,000,000 rubles.

The *Ural Region* will likewise be assigned an important task in the field of chemical development. The supply of raw materials in this region is excellent (pyrites, phosphates, potassium, etc.), the fuel resources are adequate and, besides, the greatest possibilities exist in the utilization of the by-products of non-ferrous metal smelting, coking and coal combustion. In the chemical, as well as in the metallurgical and machine-building fields, the Ural region has the great task of providing the driving force for the industrial development, not only of the adjoining districts, but also of Western Siberia and Central Asia.

The first large chemical combine in the Urals will be built in the Bereznikov district, the Kizel coal deposits being utilized as the source of energy. This enterprise, of a total estimated cost of 60,000,000 rubles, will have a capacity of about 260,000 tons of soda ash by the end of the five-year period (in 1927-28 the total output in the Soviet Union was 208,000 tons) and of 350,000 tons of acid phosphate (or also more than the total production of the country in 1927-28). The second fertilizer establishment in the Ural region will be in the Saldinsk district. It will utilize the coke gases of the district, the sulphuric acid derived as a by-product of the Bogomolov copper smelters and, finally, the Viatka phosphate deposits. The annual capacity of this plant will be brought up to about 150,000 metric tons of sulphuric acid and 350,000 tons of phosphates (in equivalent of standard superphosphate). The total cost is estimated at approximately 25,000,000 rubles. A third fertilizer plant in the Ural region, which will utilize the coking by-products of the Magnitogorsk plant, will produce about 40,000 tons of ammonia to be converted into high grade nitrate fertilizers for the use of the cotton growers in Central Asia. The cost of this concern has also been set at about 25,000,000 rubles. A similar or somewhat larger outlay will be required for the organization of potash production from the Solikamsk deposits. One or two mines (the first in the Soviet Union) will be completed during the five-year period, with an aggregate output of 1.5 million tons of potassium salts per year. At the same time, it is planned to construct in this region three or four plants for wood distillation, each to have an output (of acetic acid, methyl alcohol, etc.) larger than the present total for the country as a whole. In other words, here too the foundation is being laid for an entirely new industry.

The total amount to be invested in the Ural chemical industry is about 230,000,000 rubles.

In Siberia and the Far East the object to be attained in the next five years, is not so much the actual development of a chemical industry as a thorough and complete investigation of the local opportunities in this field, to serve as a basis for the development program for the following five-year period. That the opportunities are considerable is indicated by the results of the first prospecting explorations and, in particular, by the discovery in 1928 of salt lakes with rich reserves of self-precipitated salt. These, however, will be utilized for industrial purposes in the five-year period only to a limited extent (about 60,000 tons of salt). At the same time, with the development of coke production in the Kusnetz Basin, it will be possible to establish a large plant for the production of a number of chemicals, and the enormous timber reserves will permit at least the initial steps to be taken in the development of a wood-distillation industry in Siberia. The capital to be invested in the Siberian chemical industry is estimated at 70,000,000 rubles in five years.

In Central Asia the situation with regard to the exploration of resources is about the same as in Siberia. One of the most important phases of the chemical problem in this region is the Kara-Bugas project, where, however, it will not be expedient to bring the industrial output of sulphates above a limited amount—about 70,000 tons per year by the end of the five-year period. In addition, Central Asia is confronted with the problem of creating a large plant for the production of mineral fertilizers, to utilize the Chirchik electric power and, possibly, the important phosphate deposits in the Aktubinsk district. The total investments in the chemical industry in Central Asia are estimated at about 70,000,000 rubles for the period.

The most cursory examination of the development program of the chemical industry, for the country as a whole and for the several regions, can leave no doubt but that we have here *an entirely new and extremely difficult sector of the construction front.* The accomplishment of the tasks outlined within such a limited time will constitute a genuine triumph for the skilled working corps to whom they have been entrusted and will mark an enormous advance on the road to the economic upbuilding of the country.

6. PRODUCTION OF BUILDING MATERIALS

The experience of the past few years has shown that the production of building materials is one of the Soviet industries where system and organization are at a low level of efficiency. This has resulted in greatly retarding and, at times, even completely disorganizing the work on the various development projects. Therefore, one of the most serious tasks of the five-year development program is to make such provisions in regard to the production of building materials as will assure unobstructed progress for the entire construction plan, raise the quality of materials, and guarantee the accumulation of the necessary stocks. The development of the building materials industry will be effected through the combination of large plants in the vicinity of the more important construction projects and the maximum utilization of the abundant opportunities for small-scale production, to provide for the needs of local construction activities.

The five-year plan provides for a total investment of about 860,000,000 rubles for the *organization and development of the production of building materials,* this including only production for the needs of industries regulated by the Supreme Council of National Economy.

As a result of these investments the production of the basic building materials will increase as follows:

	1927-28	*1932-33*	*Ratio of 1932-33 to 1927-28 Per Cent*
Cement (millions of barrels)	11.9	40.0	336.1
Bricks (billions of units)	1.8	9.3	516.7
Asbestos (thousands of tons)	26	150	576.9
Sawmill products (millions of cubic meters)	11.6	42.5	366.4

A comparison of this growth in the production of building materials with the scale of capital investments in the leading branches of national economy, as provided under the plan, indicates that by the end of the five-year period, a steady and adequate supply of materials will be assured. The first years of the period, however (and especially the year 1929-30), will witness a shortage of building materials. For this reason the success of the development program demands that additional funds, and, what is even more important, additional organizational efforts, be expended on this industry before the expiration of the current year.

It should be emphasized that the success or failure of the general construction program, especially in regard to the lowering of costs, will depend to a great degree upon the extent to which the methods of large-scale industry are introduced, both into the production of building materials (simplification, standardization, etc.) and into the building trades. The fact must be frankly faced that in these matters the Soviet Union is still very backward, and that rapid progress in this respect is one of the most essential prerequisites for the success of the development program as a whole.

7. FORESTRY AND THE LUMBER INDUSTRY

The tasks in this field are defined by the programs for the wood-treating industries (production of cellulose, paper, wood distillation, artificial silk, etc.) and for lumber exports.

The unfavorable geographical distribution of forests in the Soviet Union greatly complicates the problem of preparing the required timber area for exploitation. Its solution is closely connected with the problems of assisted migration and development of the transportation system.

While the total forest area in the Soviet Union, aside from that of purely local importance, is 877.3 million hectares, only 157.5 million, or 17.7 per cent of the total, were under exploitation on October 1, 1928, to which will be added by 1932-33 an additional 35.6 million hectares, that is, 22 per cent of the area now under exploitation. The production of timber in the exploited area amounted in 1927-28 to 142.5 million cubic meters, including 60.7 million cubic meters of wood, or 42.6 per cent of the total, for further transformation. In 1932-33 the timber production is to attain a total of 258.1 million cubic meters, of which 48.4 per cent (124.8 million cubic meters) will go for reworking. Thus, parallel with the process of extending the forest area under exploitation, there will be an increase in the utilization of the area (intensification of forest development) and also an increase in the production of timber for further working, as a result of the growth of the cellulose and paper and wood-distillation industries.

The amount and distribution of capital investments in forestry are dictated by the following program of work: (a) preparation of forest area for exploitation, through forest organization and economic investigation; (b) increasing the productivity of forests through reforestation of wastes, draining of swampy lands and care of young growth; (c) development of lumber transportation, through the construction of forest highways and of outlets for rafting, and (d) reclamation of forests and lands through afforestation of sands and ravines, establishment of windbreaks, shelter belts for protection against snow, etc. The total capital invested in forestry in 1927-28 was 12.8 million rubles and the investments for the five-year period are estimated at about 247,000,000 rubles.

The five-year program of forestry development for the several constituent republics is shown in the table on the page opposite.

The carrying out of these measures will create a basis for the proper development of the lumber industry, in accordance with the needs of construction, of the cellulose and paper industries, wood distillation, and the lumber export trade. The gross production of the lumber industry will increase 275 per cent in the five-year period, and the output of sawmills for building requirements, 267 per cent. The principal centers of development will be the North East region (sawmill output of 6.6 million cubic meters a year, with an increase of 343 per cent in the five years), the Urals (output of 2.0 million cubic meters, increase of 431 per cent), the Lower Volga region (output of 7.4 million cubic meters, increase of 746 per cent), and the Far East (output of 2.1 million cubic meters, increase 700 per cent).

In the North East Region, the Urals and the Far East, the sawmill industry is combined with the production of cellulose and paper, as well as with wood distillation (the latter especially in the Urals). This

FIVE-YEAR PROGRAM OF FORESTRY DEVELOPMENT

	Units of Measurement	Total for Union of Socialist Soviet Republics	Constituent Republics: Russian Socialist Federated Soviet Republic	Ukrainian Socialist Soviet Republic	White Russian Socialist Soviet Republic	Transcaucasian Socialist Federated Soviet Republic	Republics of Central Asia
(1) Amount of timber production	millions						
1927-28	of cubic	142.5	127.7	4.0	8.4	2.0	0.4
1932-33	meters	258.1	239.2	5.5	9.0	3.5	0.9
Increase over 1927-28	per cent	81.1	87.3	37.5	7.1	75.0	125.0
(2) Forest area under exploitation (state forests)	millions						
1927-28	of	157.5	146.7	2.6	2.7	1.9	3.6
1932-33	hectares	193.1	180.0	2.6	3.2	2.8	4.5
Increase over 1927-28	per cent	22.6	22.7	....	18.5	47.4	25.0
(3) Capital investments in forestry							
1927-28	millions	12.8	8.4	2.5	1.3	0.3	0.3
1928-29 to 1932-33 (incl.)	of rubles	246.9	174.2	38.3	16.5	10.0	7.9

combination assures the greatest returns on the capital investments allotted to those regions. In the Lower Volga Region sawmilling is combined with wood-working industries, and here it is planned to utilize, in particular, sawmill waste products (which will amount, according to estimates, to nearly 2.5 million cubic meters) for the production of wall and building slabs by the methods lately introduced in the United States. In the other forest regions having a developed lumber industry (as for instance the White Russian Republic) the changes planned are in the direction of expanding the woodworking industries and, particularly, the production of building details.

The construction of new mills in the four principal lumber regions (North East, Ural, Lower Volga and Far East) will require an outlay of 176,000,000 rubles, which is 47 per cent of the total amount to be invested in the lumber industry (375,000,000 rubles).

The program will provide for the production of lumber for export in amounts greatly exceeding the present lumber exports of the Soviet Union. The main lumber exporting regions in 1932-33 will be Karelia and the North East, and the Far East; the Urals will supply high grade lumber for export, chiefly from the eastern portion of the region; Siberia is expected to develop lumber exports by way of the Kara Sea; the Transcaucasian republics and White Russia will export special classes of hardwoods and manufactured wood products.

8. THE DEVELOPMENT PROGRAM FOR INDUSTRY AS A WHOLE

Above has been given a general outline of the development program of the most important branches of industry. It is impossible to discuss here a number of other industries which, though of considerable importance, will not require capital construction of such magnitude, nor undergo such a thoroughgoing reorganization as the above-mentioned industries. This applies, primarily, to the "light industry" group. Although the basic capital of these industries is considerable at the present time, this *will have to be increased by about 2.9 billion rubles in the five-year period* (including investment of 1.1 billion rubles in the textile industry, and 0.7 billion rubles in the food and allied industries). These investments are dictated by the necessity of gradually eliminating the goods famine in the country.

The total amount to be invested in the basic capital of the state industries regulated by the Supreme Council of National Economy, including equipment and installation, is about 13.5 billion rubles. Adding those industries not thus regulated, and also investments in industrial housing construction, the investments in industry for the five-year period will amount to 16.4 billion rubles. In accordance with the general policy of industrialization of the country, the industries of "Group A," i.e., the producers' goods industries, will receive, out of the total, 9.8 billion rubles, while "Group B," i.e., industries producing consumers' goods, will receive 2.9 billions. There should further be added to the investments in "Group A" an amount of about 610 million rubles for research, geological explorations, planning bureaus, etc.

The indicated investments in state industry and the development program they represent will mean, of course, not only an expansion in the volume of industrial production and an increase in industry's share in the total production of the country, but also a considerable improvement in industrial efficiency.

As will be shown below in greater detail, by 1932-33 the output of industry regulated by the Supreme Council of National Economy will, as a result of these outlays, increase 180 per cent as compared with 1927-28, and *about 35 per cent of the total industrial output will come from newly constructed plants, not including old establishments reconstructed or reequipped.* If the unregulated industries are included, the industrial output in 1932-33 will be 136 per cent above that of 1927-28.

The share of industry in the total net production of the country, that is, in the national income, will increase from 32 per cent at the beginning of the five-year period to 34 per cent at the end. This change is particularly significant when it is considered that it will take place simultaneously with a rapid growth of agricultural production.

The cost of industrial production will be reduced 35 per cent in the five years, and, as has been stated above, construction costs will be reduced 50 per cent. The decline in the total construction index is expected to come to 28 per cent.

The power equipment of industry will increase greatly in the course of the five years. Whereas the industrial consumption of mechanical power in 1927-28 was 1.24 kilowatt-hours per man hour, in 1932-33 it will be 2.61 kilowatt-hours per man hour, that is, more than twice as large.

It is thus quite evident that the five-year program for the upbuilding of state industry will mark a considerable advance in the process of raising the Soviet Union to the level of the advanced capitalistic countries and will provide a basis for even more rapid progress in the great competitive race between socialist and capitalist economy.

9. RECONSTRUCTION PROBLEMS AND OUTLINE OF DEVELOPMENT WORK IN AGRICULTURE

The decree of the Central Executive Committee of the U.S.S.R. in regard to the increase of crop yields, has clearly mapped out the road for agricultural progress in the Soviet Union. Supplying agriculture with technical equipment through the aid of industry, improvement of the status of the lower and middle peasant groups, accelerated development of state farming on a large scale, of collective farming organizations, and of cooperative associations, raising of the cultural level of the peasantry as a whole,—such are the problems to be faced. These problems are only different aspects of the general object to be attained, which is the rapid growth of productive forces of the village and its organization along socialistic lines on the basis of machine technique and scientific cultivation of land. The development program in agriculture has been drawn up in accordance with these general objectives.

The total to be invested in agriculture during the five-year period has been set at 23 billion rubles, including private investments of individual peasant households (in buildings, live-stock, implements, etc.). Of the total investments, about 9 or 10 billion rubles will be, to a greater or less extent, subject to the direct regulation and control of the state. Finally, about 5.8 billion rubles will be a direct investment of the state in agriculture, whether coming from the government budget or from credit grants.[1]

Within the limits of these general investments, the development program for agriculture may now be described.

The outstanding phase of that program and the one that determines its entire character is the *upbuilding, on a scale heretofore unknown, of the socialized sector in agriculture.* In view of the tremendous importance of this object in the general system of economic and

[1] The figures given here have been calculated at constant prices. The actual amount of financing, taking into consideration the reduction in prices, will be 5.1 billion rubles.

social relationships in the Soviet Union, the task assigned to that sector in the program represents nearly the maximum that can be achieved in the five-year period. The program provides for an extension of the planted area in the socialized sector from 2.3 million hectares in 1927-28 to 26,000,000 by 1933, of which 5,000,000 hectares will be in state farms and 21 million in collective farms. Of the total sum of 5.8 billion rubles to be invested in agriculture, about 2 billion (at constant prices) will go into state and collective farms. As a result, *the socialized sector as a whole will supply, by the end of the period (crop of 1932), 19.8 per cent of the total and 43 per cent of the marketable portion of the grain crop* (exclusive of sales to peasants).

Finally, as giving an indication of the scale of the development expected in this field, it should be pointed out that, by the end of the period, collective farms will include about 20,000,000 persons, or about 6,000,000 peasant households, which will mean that *the peasant population in households outside of the collective farming system will remain practically stable,* while the agricultural population as a whole will be steadily and rapidly increasing. The development plan for agriculture will also provide a solution of the acute problem, now confronting the country, of eliminating the disturbances and partial crises in agricultural production which have been witnessed in the past two years. Only a decisive advance along the road of socialist reconstruction of the village will open up real opportunities for overcoming the low productivity of small scale farming and for assuring widespread agricultural progress.

From the point of view of the reorganization of farming the socialized sector of the agricultural front is of particular interest in that it is based entirely upon machine technique, the wide application of mineral fertilizers, the introduction of tractors, and in general, upon improvement and scientific methods. It is sufficient to point out that at the end of the five-year period there will be about 170,000 tractors in use in this sector (including about 30,000 at tractor service stations), that state and collective farms will acquire about 863,000,000 rubles' worth of agricultural machinery during the period, that chemical fertilizers will be used on a considerable portion of the area under cultivation and selected seeds on about 60 per cent of the area. As a result of this reconstruction program, *the crop yield in the socialized sector is expected to increase twice as fast as the yield for agriculture as a* whole.

The newness of this undertaking, the absence of any real experience in foreign countries by which to be guided (even as far as large-scale farming practice is concerned, let alone the collective organization of agriculture), the specific difficulties of a social nature due to the very low cultural level of the country and, finally, the enormous scope of the work planned, all demand that the most strenuous efforts and careful supervision be exercised in order to carry out the program for developing the socialized sector.

Unusual difficulties are involved in the problem of reorganizing farming on a collective basis and of devising such forms of collective organization as will guarantee the maximum effectiveness of the capital invested. The fact must be frankly faced that in this field we are still feeling our way, that the fundamental technical principles of collective farming have not as yet been clearly formulated. *The guiding practical idea behind the organizational form of collective farming should be that of central machinery and tractor stations serving a group of villages, and of their eventual transformation into centers of power supply and agricultural aid in a broad sense.* This idea has already been partially applied in the Ukraine, with satisfactory results. It opens up a new chapter in the power base and in the technical and social reconstruction of agriculture. Only through a development of this character is the possibility presented of rapidly and systematically extending the mechanical resources of peasant labor, on which depends the solution of the central problem of agricultural progress. Only in this manner can be secured a solid technical basis of genuine collectivization, embracing the masses of the poor and middle peasantry.

The most ambitious part of the development program is that relating to the organization of agricultural territory, that is, to land organization, reclamation, irrigation, etc.

The general scope of the program of *land organization* is indicated by the following figures:

	Total Area to be Organized (Millions of hectares)	*Land Organization in Five Years*	*Total Land Organization to be Completed by the end of the Five-year Period*
		Per Cent of Total Area	
1. Land organization among individual peasant holdings	149	37.5	80.6
2. Elimination or decrease of distant holdings	69	17.2	60.5
3. Elimination of strip holdings,	138	54.8	75.0
Of which in collective farms	35	13.8	16.1
4. Crop rotation	110	56.5	56.5
5. State farms	14	100.0	100.0
6. Lands assigned to cities, government departments or enterprises, for special purposes	3.5	....	....

The total cost of land organization in the five years has been estimated at 524,000,000 rubles at constant prices, or, allowing for reduction of costs, at 490,000,000 rubles. But the crux of the problem of land organization is, perhaps, not so much the scale of the work to be accomplished as the necessity of establishing it on a new basis and of finding new approaches to the problem, conforming with the great tasks of socialization and mechanization of agricultural production. *In the five-year period a transition must be made from the systemless land organization of the past, which was done at the request of individual villages, to the organization of large tracts of farming territory in accordance with a general plan.* In those districts where mechanization of agriculture will be introduced, *land organization should be centered around the machine and tractor service stations* mentioned above. The plan of land organization will, of course, also be closely linked up with the new programs of road construction and development of motor transportation, which will inevitably follow the widespread introduction of tractors and machines in agriculture.

Reclamation work in the five-year period will cover an area of over 2,000,000 hectares, not including the large irrigation projects in Central Asia and Transcaucasia connected with cotton growing. About 80 per cent of the reclamation work will consist of drainage operations, with a view to increasing the feed crop acreage in regions where intensive stock raising is carried on. About 400,000 hectares will be embraced by the irrigation program, chiefly flood irrigation in the arid regions along the Turkestan-Siberian Railway. Finally, experimental irrigation will be undertaken over an area of some 30,000 hectares in the Volga region, marking the beginning of irrigation work in that district, and preliminary explorations for large irrigation projects in the Lower Dnieper region will be continued.

The estimated cost of land reclamation during the five-year period is about 530,000,000 rubles (at constant prices), of which about 347,000,000 rubles will be provided from state resources. Making allowance for reduction in costs, the plan of general financing provides an amount of about 490,000,000 rubles, including 320,000,000 rubles from the State Treasury.

The general scope of irrigation work connected with cotton growing may be seen from the following figures:

	Increase in the Five-year Period (thousands of hectares)			*Cost of Irrigation in the Five-year Period (millions of rubles)*	
	Irrigated	*Improved*	*Planted to Cotton*	*Not Including Private Resources of the Population*	*Including Private Resources of the Population*
Central Asia and Kazak Autonomous Socialist Soviet Republic	1,191	1,037	640	303	343
Of which, large-scale projects.	655	508	247	241	261
Transcaucasian Socialist Federated Soviet Republic	473	430	122	127	136
Of which, large-scale projects	311	270	77	95	99
Total	1,664	1,467	762	430	479
Of which, large-scale projects.	966	778	324	336	360

The five-year plan is based on the necessity of increasing domestic cotton production to 1.91 million metric tons, which will almost completely do away with the dependence of the Soviet Union upon imported cotton, and thus release funds for the import of industrial equipment. The great importance of this task, the scope and the urgency of the irrigation work, the amount of capital invested, and the very inadequate scientific and technical organization in this field at the present time, demand that serious and sustained attention be devoted to it. The entire program of irrigation in connection with cotton growing must be given as great consideration by the controlling organs during the whole of the five-year period as such undertakings as the Dnieprostroy, development of the metal industry, etc.

It is unnecessary to stress the fact that among the problems connected with agricultural territory, the task of adding some 12 to 15 million hectares to the area under cultivation, as provided under the plan, is of the greatest importance. This program, which is dependent on the mechanization of agriculture, will mean a considerable extension of the planted acreage in the Volga region and in the eastern part of the country.

At the same time, another new factor in agriculture, namely, the application of chemical methods, will afford an approach to the question of extending the area under cultivation in the consuming agricultural zone (the territory which now has to purchase grain from other regions), by making available waste lands and unproductive local forests. This will, of course, require proper coordination with the plans relating to forestry.

One of the most important weapons in the reconstruction of agriculture and of peasant economy is the five-year *program of machine supply.* This provides for an increase in the amount of agricultural machinery in the country from about one billion rubles in value, at the beginning of the five-year period, to 2.4 billions at the end, or, including tractors, to about 3 billion rubles. Inasmuch as during the period the intensity of utilization of agricultural machines will be greatly increased, with the development of the socialized sector, *the actual capacity of the mechanical equipment in agriculture will not increase three-fold, but considerably more.* In the plan of agricultural reconstruction the extension of the use of machinery, on the one hand, and of collective and cooperative methods, on the other, are intimately connected, as two aspects of a general process of technical and social reconstruction of farming. The mechanization of agriculture is an instrument in the socialist reorganization of peasant life, the handling of which is a task of special importance and responsibility.

Finally, an important *new force will enter the field of agricultural reconstruction in the shape of the newly organized chemical industry of the Soviet Union.* At the present time the Soviet Union ranks among the most backward countries in regard to the use of mineral fertilizers, of which it produces only an insignificant quantity. By the end of the five-year period agriculture will be obtaining 7,000,000 tons of mineral fertilizers a year, and the Soviet Union will occupy a much more prominent place among the leading agricultural countries in this respect. Mineral fertilizers will be applied to the entire cotton, sugar beet and flax area, to over 6 per cent of the total area planted to grain, and to 25 per cent of the grain acreage in the socialized sector. The significance of this factor in increasing agricultural production will be further enhanced by the effect which the use of fertilizers may have in extending the grain acreage to lands in the central regions, now lying idle.

Of special significance in connection with agricultural reconstruction is the group of enterprises, connected with the *industrialization of agriculture,* which are engaged in the transformation of agricultural products. The capital investments in this group in the half-decade will amount to about 1.5 billion rubles, including about 350,000,000 rubles in the sugar industry, 200,000,000 rubles in flour milling, 150,000,000 rubles in the dairy and meat industries, 125,000,000 rubles in poultry raising and egg production, 75,000,000 rubles in the flax, hemp and kenaf industries, and about 60,000,000 rubles in fruit growing and truck gardening. The total output of industries working up agricultural products will increase in the five-year period from 1.2 billion rubles to about 3.5 billions. In this field, also, important problems of organization arise, the solution of which should eventually lead to increased importance of collective and cooperative groups in the development of these industries.

In all these measures for the upbuilding of agriculture, the importance of *a proper selection* and an adequate supply of *pure strain seeds* is self-evident. In this connection a leading part will be played by the State Farms, which are expected to become nurseries for the breeding of high-grade seeds on a large scale and to provide sustenance for the systematic improvement of the seed resources of peasant economy.

The above are the outstanding features in the development program for agriculture. They do not, of course, in any way diminish the importance of the very simple and effective measures for improving farming methods which were discussed in detail in the explanatory statement accompanying the decree of the Central Executive Committee of the Soviet Union on the increase of crop yields. It is obvious that the effectiveness of the ambitious projects outlined in the plan will be completely or, at least, partially nullified unless they are accompanied by a rise in the production level and a furthering of the interests and the efforts of the millions of poor and middle peasants. Only the combination of these great projects together with the struggling efforts of the peasant masses can achieve the aims provided in the plan, which include an increase of almost 23 per cent in the total area under cultivation, a 25 per cent increase in the yield per acre during the remaining four years of the period covered by the plan, an increase in the gross volume and in the marketable portion of agricultural output, etc.

There are, of course, special *regional problems* in regard to agriculture, none of which have been pointed out in the preceding outline. In a very general way it may be stated that the measures taken for the building up of the socialized sector and the development of grain farming will bring about a considerable increase in the relative importance of the eastern districts and, to some extent, of the Volga region, while the relative importance of the Ukraine and of Northern Caucasus in the agricultural production of the country as a whole will become somewhat less, notwithstanding the growth of their production in absolute amounts. By the end of the five-year period the Ukraine and Northern Caucasus will no longer serve as sources of grain supply for the central regions but will become primarily producers of grain for export, whereas the supply of the central regions will come from the Volga district and from the districts further east, located at considerable distance from the Black Sea ports.

The rate of increase in production and in the yield per acre to be effected as a result of the development program for agriculture, is convincing evidence of the thoroughness and effectiveness of the measures planned in order to make these advances possible.

10. PROGRAM OF RECONSTRUCTION AND OF NEW DEVELOPMENT IN TRANSPORTATION

The growth of production provided under the plan, and the accompanying development of new regions, will, naturally, result in heavy demands upon transportation in general and railways in particular. On the fulfillment of these demands will depend in a great measure the successful realization of the five-year plan.

Of special significance in its bearing on trade, and on the program of reconstruction and new development, will be railway transportation. Its problems must, therefore, be given first place in a discussion of the projects planned in this field.

The primary importance of railway transportation is reflected in the distribution of the capital investments provided for the five-year period for the various forms of transportation. Of the total of 10 billion rubles which is to be invested in transportation during the period, over 6.7 billions will go into railways. Of this amount, about 60 per cent is assigned for the reconstruction of existing railways and about 40 per cent for new railway construction. *Reconstruction of existing railways thus constitutes the dominant part of the entire development program in transportation.*

The first element in the reorganization of the railways will be the replacement of the greater part of the existing freight locomotives by high-powered (80 tons) locomotives of the new series "E." This will require the introduction of over 3,000 of the new locomotives. In addition, as an experiment to prepare for the performance of tasks which will arise during the succeeding period, it is planned to introduce 35 locomotives of a higher capacity (100 tons).

The second element of reconstruction will be the increase of freight-car equipment through the addition of some 160,000 units (two-axle cars or equivalent). At the same time the proportion of large capacity cars will be increased during the period from 5 per cent of the whole number to 20 per cent, by increasing their number to 60,000 units. There will also be a growth in the number of gondola cars and flat cars.

The third important task in the reorganization program is the introduction of *automatic coupling.* As a result of a thorough investigation of this problem it has been decided to confine the work during the five years under consideration to preparatory measures (selection of type of automatic couplers, placing of orders, adjusting of cars, testing of couplers over blocked routes, such as the roads from Donetz to Krivoy-Rog, or from Magnitnaya to Kuznetz Basin), with a view to having the transfer to the new couplers entirely accomplished in the succeeding five-year period.

The fourth item relates to *automatic brakes* on freight trains, the introduction of which will be fully completed in the course of the five years.

As an extension of previous experiments it is planned to substitute oil for steam locomotives on the stretch from Stalingrad to Tikhoretzkaya, where the water supply is deficient.

Finally, electrification of railways will be carried out during the period on the suburban sections of the railways converging at Moscow, at the Suramsk pass on the Transcaucasian railways, on the Mineralniye Vody branch, on the Kiselov branch in the Urals and on the Liman-Kharkov line. Great efforts will be required before the idea of railway electrification becomes firmly assimilated as a part of the practical program of transportation development in the Soviet Union. And while the railway reconstruction program for the five-year period may appear rather modest at first glance, it involves considerable difficulties and its realization will mark a considerable advance in railway development. It is sufficient to indicate that, when it has been carried out, transportation costs will be reduced by some 20 per cent on the average. For this reason the program of investments for the reconstruction of existing railways must be fulfilled in its entirety.

An analysis of the prospective flow of freight traffic for the five-year period forcefully suggests that on two of the leading arteries of commerce the traffic will, by the end of the period, either be nearly approaching the limit of the capacity of the roads, or will have exceeded it. The lines here indicated are those connecting the Donetz Basin with Moscow and with Leningrad, and the lines running to Siberia. These lines constitute the big transportation problem of the country. The problem of concentrating freight movement and radically reducing the costs of moving large cargoes will loom with especial acuteness. Both from the standpoint of general economic reconstruction and, in particular, of transportation development, the only correct solution of this problem is the concentration of freight traffic on the reorganized or newly built super-trunk lines. The problem, however, cannot be solved in the coming five years. During this period the problem will be approached from two angles. The method of scattered freight movement will still be used or even extended, while preparatory work will be carried on for the transformation of the lines concerned into super-trunk lines.

With an outlay of some 100,000,000 rubles for the extension of junctions, additional track laying, automatic signals, etc., and with the construction of a few new lines, the freight movement between the Donetz Basin and Moscow and between the Donetz Basin and Leningrad may be assured during the five-year period by the method of scattered traffic. No material reduction in transportation costs will thus be obtained, however. This solution is the only available one for the time being, inasmuch as the projects involved in converting these lines into super-trunk lines (electrification of the Kursk railway, completion of the super-trunk line Moscow-Voronezh-Donetz Basin) have not yet been worked out in final shape. The plan provides, however, for an appropriation of about 70,000,-

000 rubles for completing preparatory investigations and beginning actual work by the end of the five-year period, so that the project may be entirely carried out in the succeeding five years.

As regards the Siberian trunk line and the outlets from Siberia towards Moscow and Leningrad, the freight traffic on these routes is expected to exceed the carrying capacity of the existing lines by the end of the period. A thorough study of this problem has demonstrated the *exceptional, in fact overwhelming, economic importance of providing a super-trunk line for the Siberian traffic.* The five-year plan contains a series of projects which will constitute a gradual approach to the solution of the problem. In the first three years there will be completed the construction of the new Kurgan-Sverdlovsk line, with the reconstruction of the existing section, Sinarskoye-Shadrinsk. The new line is projected with an easy grade, and in a similar manner a grade revision will also be effected on the Kurgan-Novosibirsk section of the Siberian trunk line. In this connection there is a further provision for the construction of a second track on the Sverdlovsk-Shemordan section of the Kazan railway, west of the Urals, and for a new line from Shemordan to Nizhni-Novgorod, with a double-track bridge over the Volga. The total costs of these projects in the five-year period will be about 220,000,000 rubles.

Along with this program of railway reconstruction

there is a plan for the construction of new railways. At the present time the railway mileage of the Soviet Union is 77,000 kilometers, which is more than 30 per cent above the mileage operated in the same territory in 1913. An additional 3,600 kilometers is under construction. During the course of the five-year period it is planned to begin construction on 22,600 kilometers of railways, and to put 17,000 kilometers into operation. The total length of operating lines will thus be raised to 94,000 kilometers.

The program of new railway construction for the period in its most important aspects may be summarized as follows: (See map on pages 100-101.)

(a) *New lines designed primarily for lumber transportation and, partly, for the colonization of undeveloped regions,* will have a total mileage of about 2,800 kilometers, and will include, among others, a line connecting the Central Industrial Region with the Pechora region, the central section of which, running from Ust-Sysolsk to Kotlas, will be completed in the course of the five years; the first portion of a large lumber-carrying trunk line from Soroka to Kotlas, to serve the export trade; the Yenisei road in Siberia, and a number of secondary lumber roads in the western part of European Russia, the Urals, the Caucasus and the Far East.

(b) *New lines serving agriculture and, partly, colonization of undeveloped regions,* will have a mileage of about 6,800 kilometers. Of these, the most important

MURMANSK
SOROKA
ARKHANGELSK
PETROZAVODSK
LENINGRAD
KOTLAS
UST-SISOLSK
IVDEL
PSKOV
NOVGOROD
SUDA
SOLIKAMSK
VESIEGONSK
GALICH
VIATKA
GLAZOV
KIZEL
BOLOGOE
KOSTROMA
VITEBSK
VOLOKOLAMSK
N. NOVGOROD
PERM
SVERDLOVSK
CHEBOKSARI
PAVLOVO
KAZAN
IJEVSK
MOSCOW
KANASH
GOMEL
KIEV
KURSK
UFA
SAMARA
TROITZK
SARATOV
ORSK
URALSK
AKTUBINSK
POLTAVA
DNIEPROPETROVSK
PAVLOGRAD
ODESSA
KHERSON
ROSTOV
MILLEROVO
STALINGRAD
ELISTA
DIVNOE
ASTRAKHAN
ADLER
BATUM
TIFLIS
TELAV
LENINAKAN
ARTIK
IDJEVAN
STEPANAKERT
BAKU
DJULFA
KRASNOVODSK
KHIVA

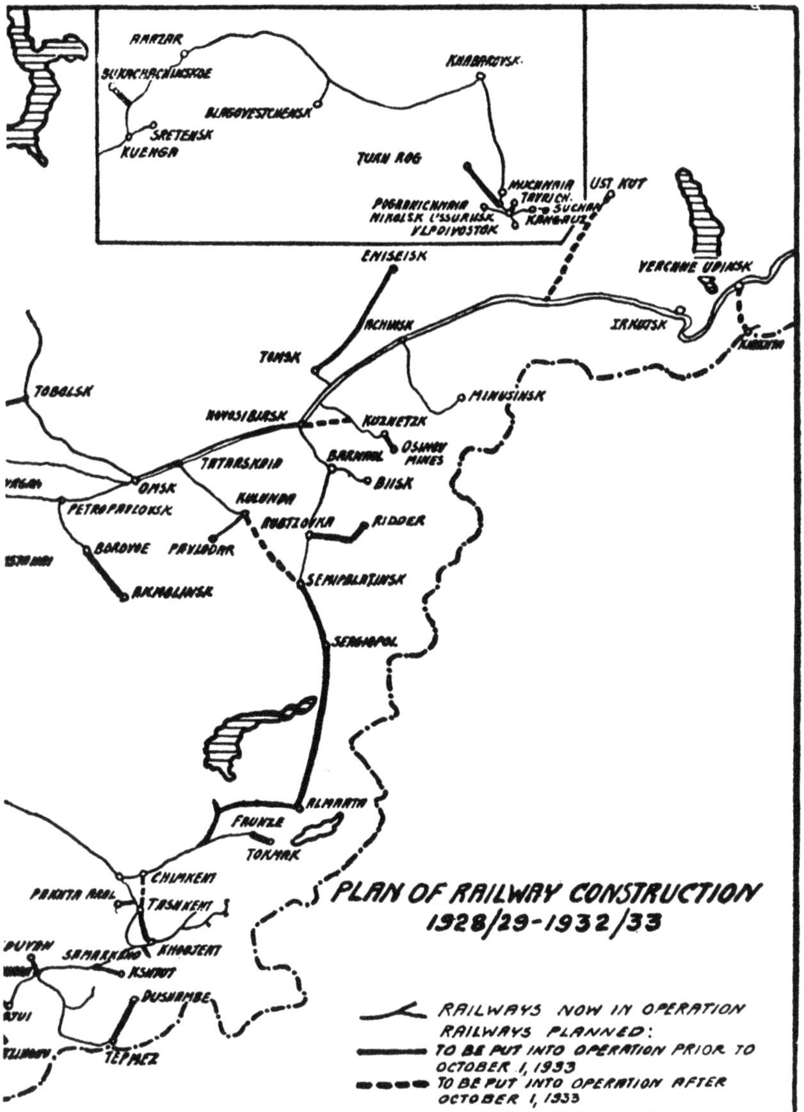

PLAN OF RAILWAY CONSTRUCTION 1928/29-1932/33

are the Turkestan-Siberian trunk line, which will be completed by the middle of the five-year period; the Borovoye-Akmolinsk and Orsk-Aktubinsk lines in the Kazak republic; a chain of agricultural lines (Troitzk-Orsk, Orenburg-Urals and Saratov-Millerovo), which together will form an inter-regional trunk system connecting the southern part of the Ural region and the Volga region with the Azov Sea ports; the big trunk line of the western part of the Ural region, which will in some sections (Perm-Ufa and Ufa-Orenburg), along with its industrial importance, have the greatest significance for agriculture; and a number of agricultural lines in the Ukraine (Armiansk-Kherson) and in Central Asia (Chardzhui-Khiva, Termes-Dushambe, and others).

(c) *New lines serving mining and manufacturing industries* will have a mileage of about 1,700 kilometers. These are designed chiefly to serve the Donetz Basin, the new coal fields in the Urals, Transcaucasia, Central Asia, and the Far East, and the districts where non-ferrous metal deposits and chemical raw materials are located (Viatka phosphorite line), etc.

(d) *New lines to take the overload of existing lines and connecting roads,* with a mileage of about 2,600 kilometers.

(e) Other new lines, 3,100 kilometers.

These are the outstanding points of the program for reconstruction and new construction of railways. This, undoubtedly, constitutes a formidable and responsible task, although the development of transportation on a scale corresponding to the needs of the Soviet Union will be possible of accomplishment only after the expiration of the five-year period, when it will be supported by more highly developed basic industries.

The predominating importance of railway transportation, which will be inevitable in the coming period, should not, however, obscure the great and difficult problems that are confronted in the development of other forms of transportation. The five-year plan provides for investments of about 180,000,000 rubles in the development of waterways and an outlay of 150,000,000 rubles for river ship construction. This will afford the possibility of strengthening the position of Soviet water transport, increasing somewhat the river traffic and concentrating it in the hands of state steamship agencies.

At the same time, *beginning with the middle of the five-year period, at least 75,000,000 rubles will be allotted for the construction of the Volga-Don Canal,* which is to be completed by the middle of the succeeding five-year period. The canal, when completed, will be of primary importance in the general water transportation system of the Soviet Union. The capital to be invested in seaports is set at 170,000,000 rubles, and in construction of seagoing vessels, 135,000,000 rubles.

A factor of great importance for the reconstruction of agriculture and the growth of its productive forces will be *the development of improved highways* in the five-year period. This is one of the weakest sectors in the economic development of the country and one of the most poorly organized. The five-year plan provides for this purpose an outlay of 400,000,000 rubles from the budget of the People's Commissariat for Transportation and for about 700,000,000 rubles from local budgets, or a total of 1.1 billion rubles. At the same time the plan strongly emphasizes the necessity of organizing this work on such a basis as shall assure the advantages that may accrue from the independent activities and the initiative of many economic organizations and of the population itself.

Finally, it is planned to invest over 100,000,000 rubles in the course of the five-year period for *the development of commercial aviation,* which is still in its infancy.

While the scale of the developments planned in transportation is smaller than in state industry, their accomplishment will nevertheless require very considerable efforts, in regard to financing and to organizational and technical measures. This program represents the strict minimum required for the period. It should be remembered that even after it has been carried out, the country's transportation facilities will still be inadequate. The program will mark, however, a considerable advance in growth of traffic, reduction of costs and the use of power. The latter point may be illustrated by the following figures showing the energy resources in transportation:

	1927-28	1932-33	Ratio of 1932-33 to 1927-28 Per Cent
Capacity of prime movers per worker (kilowatts)	6.0	8.8	146.7
Consumption of power per man-hour (kilowatt-hours)	2.05	3.11	151.7

II. PROGRAM OF HOUSING CONSTRUCTION

The housing floor space in cities (incl. industrial housing) amounts at the present time to about 160 million square meters and is valued at somewhat over 13 billion rubles, which is 18.7 per cent of the total basic capital of the country. Under the five-year construction program the housing area will be increased to 213 million square meters, of which the socialized sector will total 114 million square meters (as against 76 million at the present time). The value of all urban dwellings will accordingly increase by the end of the period to 18.5 billion rubles (at 1925-26 prices). *The total outlays for urban housing construction* (including housing in industry, electrification and transportation) *will amount for the half-decade to 5.9 billion rubles* (at prices of the respective years).

The aim of this construction program is *to increase the average housing area for the industrial population from 5.6 square meters to 7.3 square meters in the five years.* For the entire urban population the per capita housing area will be increased from 5.7 to 6.3 square meters, the per capita area remaining the same in the private sector and advancing from 5.9 to 7 square meters in the socialized sector.

During the course of the housing program the possibility must be considered, within limits of the general plan, of developing housing construction on a much larger scale in the important industrial centers which are not dependent on a large municipal economy (Donetz Basin, Ural and, partly, the Ivanovo-Voznesensk district). At all events, the housing construction program, just as every other development program, will have to be applied in accordance with specific regional needs, and must take account of the urgent problems of industrial progress.

Housing construction has, of course, its own acute problems of organization and rationalization, which are dictated by the necessity of adapting housing facilities to the new social conditions, and of adopting the best methods of American and European technique in this field. As the program is gradually carried out, there will be evolved types of inexpensive and rational dwellings corresponding to local needs. With an investment of almost 6 billion rubles in urban housing construction it is absolutely indispensable that a sufficient amount be set aside for a special institute which will bring the elements of scientific organization into this field.

Along with this program of housing construction there will also be put under way many municipal construction projects, in which a total of 2.2 billion rubles will be invested during the five-year period. Municipal construction will include, among other projects, various undertakings necessitated by the changed conditions of city life, such as public eating places, clubs, etc.

Finally, *at least a start should be made in the course of the period towards participation in the field of rural housing construction,* through the designing of a few standard types of dwellings for the various sections of the country, the organization of technical advice, and provisions for an adequate and steady supply of building materials.

12. REQUISITES OF SUCCESS OF THE FIVE-YEAR DEVELOPMENT PROGRAM

Above has been given only the outstanding features of the development program for the five-year period. Its enormous scope and the complex relationship of the component elements are quite apparent. The fundamental design of the technical and economic plan of the country in the coming period is here, and the inter-connection of its several parts stands out clearly. *It is a plan involving radical reconstruction of the production system of the country and a decisive increase in its mechanical and electrical resources as a means of industrialization and socialization.* There are scores of great projects to be carried out, conceived on a scale and in a manner dictated by the latest attainments of modern technique. It is sufficient to name such undertakings as the Dnieper River power plant and the complex of industries centering around it, the Svir River hydro-electric project, the Bobrikov central electric plant, the Turkestan-Siberian railway, the Siberian super-trunk railway, the Volga-Don canal, the series of giant metallurgical works, including the Magnitogorsk, Krivoy-Rog, Zaporozhie, Alapayev, Telbes and other steel plants, huge chemical enterprises and tractor factories, a large automobile plant, the development of great state grain farms on an unprecedented scale. *At the same time the plan will afford a tremendous test of the technical and organizational resources of the Soviet Union.* This test can and will be met in a fitting manner only on condition that all the prerequisites for carrying out the development program be thoroughly studied and fulfilled within the limits of practical possibilities.

Of these prerequisities for the success of the development program there should first be mentioned *adequate provisions and a proper organization for planning work.* The slogan of the five-year period should be the establishment of planning of the highest quality and, as a consequence, cheap and rapid construction. All the various projecting and planning organizations should, therefore, be given special attention and, in order to introduce into the Soviet Union the highest achievements of modern technique, should be afforded every opportunity for familiarizing themselves with the *latest technical attainments* of the advanced countries of Europe and America.

The Soviet Union is carrying on the unprecedented experiment of capital construction on an enormous scale financed out of current savings, with the aid of a régime of strict economy and at the sacrifice of present needs for the sake of great historical attainments. This dictates the need of extreme caution in the matter of capital investments and of the most careful scrutiny of every concrete project. It is also essential that, together with a proper organization of the planning work within the country, *the practice of engaging foreign expert aid on all important construction work be considerably extended,* organizing this engineering assistance in such a manner, however, that the work of the experts shall be a training school for the young technical personnel of the Soviet Union.

It must be further emphasized that the development program for the five-year period cannot be successfully carried out unless the entire construction work in the country is radically reorganized. *Construction work must be industrialized, it must develop into a powerful construction industry.* The great tasks set for the period cannot be successfully accomplished within so short a time if the position of the country in regard to technical knowledge remains at the comparatively low level which characterized the preceding years. The rationalization of construction work, with the utilization of the experience of the advanced industrial coun-

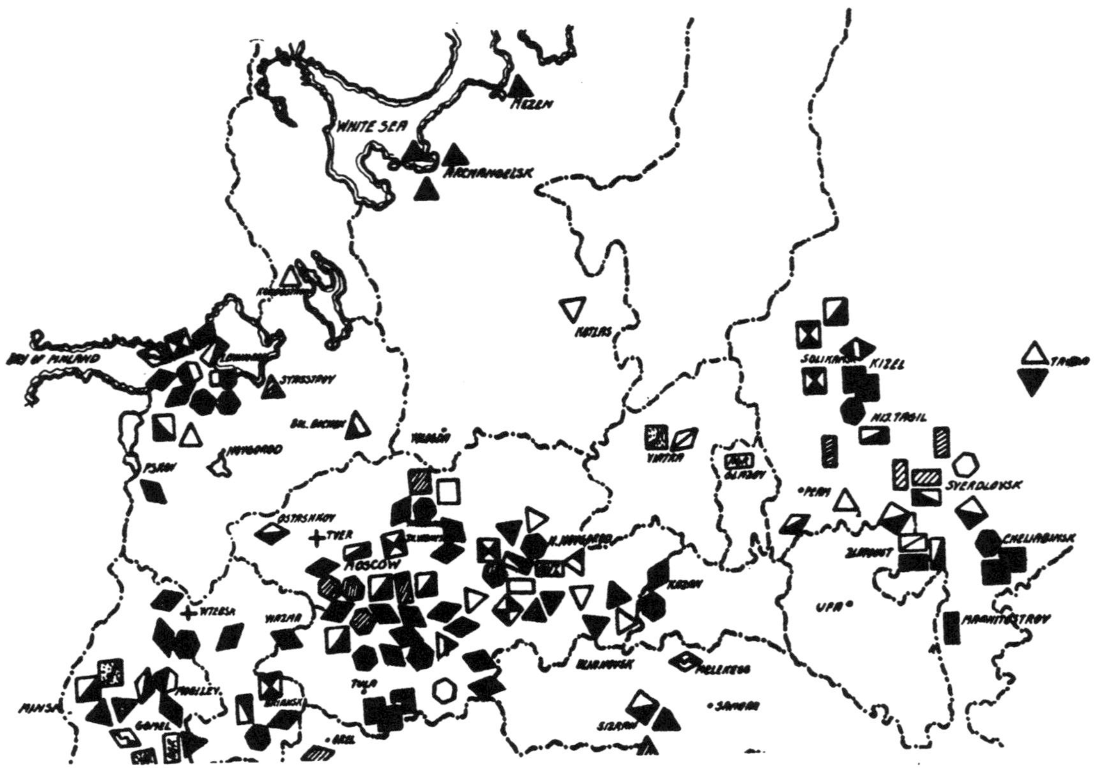
WHITE SEA
MEZEN
ARCHANGELSK
KOTLAS
BAY OF FINLAND
SYASSTROY
NOVGOROD
PSKOV
TVER
MOSCOW
N. NOVGOROD
KAZAN
VYATKA
PERM
UFA
SOLIKAMSK
KIZEL
N. TAGIL
SVERDLOVSK
CHELIABINSK
MAGNITOSTROY
TABDA
VYAZMA
VITEBSK
MINSK
MOGILEV
GOMEL
BRIANSK
ORSL
TULA
SIZRAN
SAMARA
MELEKESS
OSTASHKOV

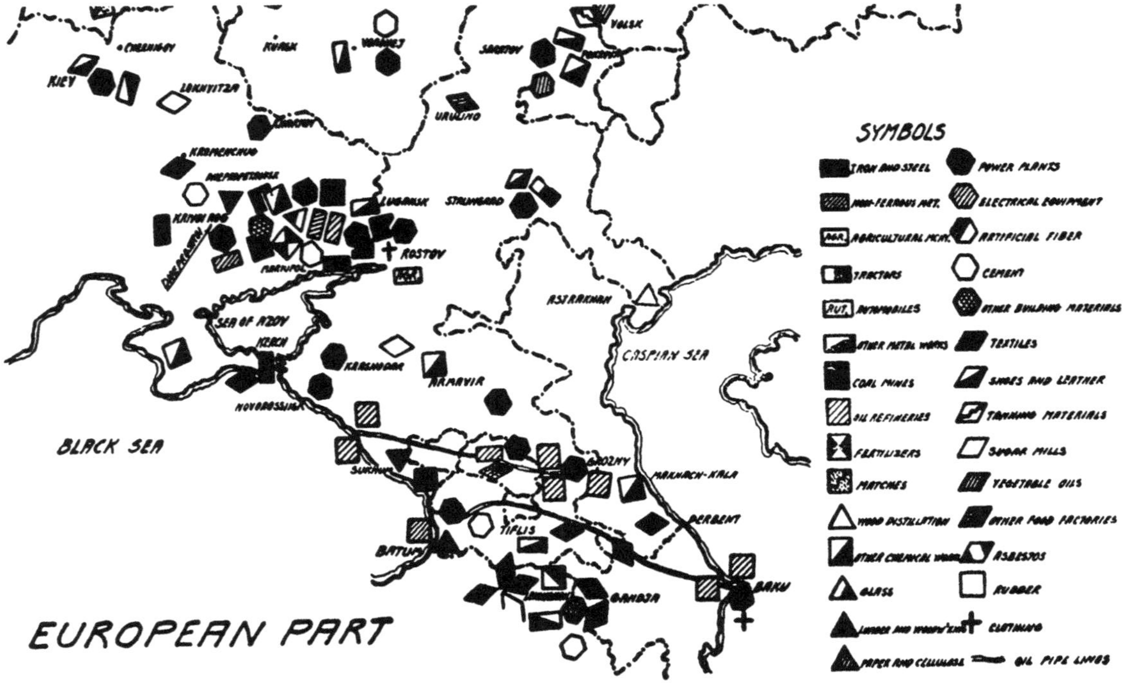

FIRST YEAR OF FIVE-YEAR PLAN
INDUSTRIAL ENTERPRISES UNDER CONSTRUCTION IN U. S. S. R., 1928-29

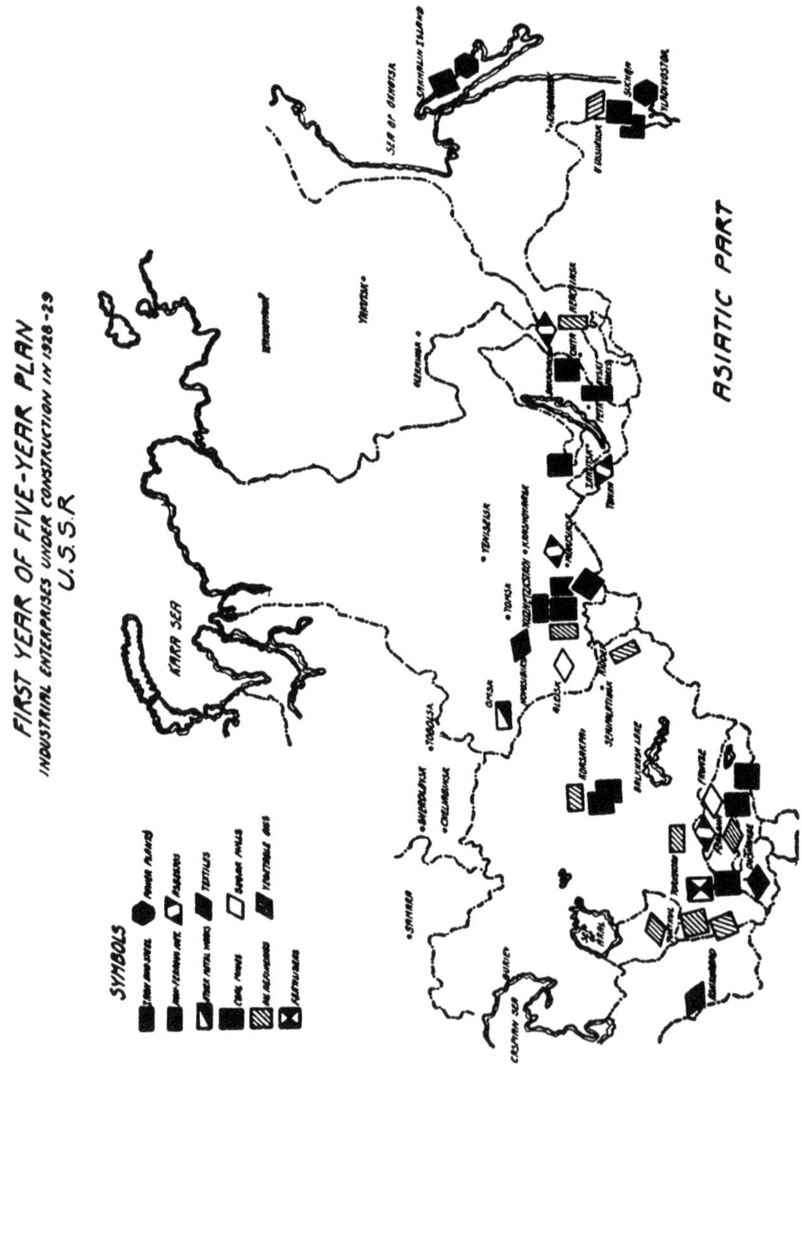
FIRST YEAR OF FIVE-YEAR PLAN
INDUSTRIAL ENTERPRISES UNDER CONSTRUCTION IN 1928-29
U.S.S.R
SYMBOLS
KARA SEA
CASPIAN SEA
SEA OF OKHOTSK
ASIATIC PART

tries, is, therefore, one of the most important prerequisites for the success of the entire plan.

As may be gathered from the preceding discussion, the development program for the five years is based upon *a further considerable extension of economic relations* with the outside world, and in particular, upon large imports of industrial equipment. For instance, the metal industry alone will require the import of equipment of a total value of about 800,000,000 rubles, and these imports will include not only individual machines, but entire aggregates of equipment or even entire departments of industrial plants. Similar demands will be made by the chemical industry, the field of electrical development and, to some extent, agriculture as well. The utmost efforts must, therefore, be exerted toward the enlargement of exports, the accumulation of foreign exchange, and the securing of long-term credits abroad in amounts far greater than at present.

The development program planned for the five-year period is unquestionably *a plan of great accomplishment,* especially when the narrow time limits are considered; it looms as a veritable battle front of reconstruction. *Only by great constructive enthusiasm and by iron discipline on this front can the great and uncommonly difficult objectives be gained.*

CHAPTER IV

THE PROBLEM OF A SKILLED LABOR FORCE

THE great development program which is designed to radically change the character and the conditions of production in the Soviet Union, and is based on the broad application of the latest and highest attainments of modern technique, naturally gives rise, in all its magnitude, to the problem of the new personnel, the new generation of workers who will be the agents of the technical and social reconstruction of the country. It may be said without exaggeration that the principal defect in the long-term planning thus far done in the Soviet Union was the failure to give due attention to this problem of personnel, and to assign to it a proper place among the primary requisites for the realization of the plans.

1. SKILLED PERSONNEL IN INDUSTRY

The question that first arises is in regard to *engineers and technicians.*[1] The number of engineers now engaged in state industry in the Soviet Union and the

[1] The term engineers as used in the Soviet Union applies to graduates of higher technical institutions, while the term technicians applies to graduates of secondary technical schools.

additional number that will be required in the five years are shown in the following table (in thousands):

	Number of Engineers Engaged in 1927-28	*Number Required in 1932-33*	*Ratio of 1932-33 to 1927-28 (Per Cent)*	*Number Engaged in 1927-28 Still Available in 1932-33*	*Number of Additional Engineers Required*
1. In production proper	13.1	32.3	246.6	10.6	21.7
2. In administrative and planning departments	7.1	9.2	129.6	5.7	3.5
Total	20.2	41.5	205.4	16.3	25.2

The existing higher technical institutions, as they now function, can supply about 20,000 engineers in the five-year period. That number, however, will have to serve not only industry but other fields as well (People's Commissariat for Transportation, construction work for commerce and transportation, teaching in vocational and technical schools, etc.). From this estimate, it can be seen that under present conditions *the shortage of engineers during the five-year period may exceed 5,000 persons.* In view of this circumstance, and also considering the great weight which other countries attach to the preparation of an engineering personnel, it is a matter of the utmost urgency that measures be undertaken to increase the number of engineers graduating from higher technical schools in the Soviet Union. It should be noted that at the present time, only about 8 per cent of all the students in these colleges graduate annually, as a number of factors combine to cause the school work to be unduly protracted. The number of graduates must be increased to at least 12 per cent, and the curriculum, the discipline, and the organization of the work must be made to conform with the great program of economic development, to serve which must be the goal of all institutions of higher learning. This, however, is not sufficient. It is necessary to investigate the question of the possibility of modifying the very system of training technical experts, in the direction of *reducing the duration of training.* While it is true that the trend of modern higher technical education is towards greater universality, and while this tendency must be duly taken into account, this does not preclude the possibility of providing intensive training for engineers in certain special fields where the shortage is most keenly felt. By means of certain modifications in their curricula, the technical schools, in particular those of the highest standing, may be helpful in covering the shortage of practical engineers.

As regards the *training of technicians*, the problem is complicated by the fact that the system of secondary technical schools which the Soviet Union inherited from the old régime was very deficient. Particular efforts must, therefore, be exerted to overcome this greatest handicap to the training of skilled workers for industry. At the present time there are about 20,000 technicians in the country. The number must be increased to 60,000 by the end of the five-year period. The existing schools can supply only about 6,000 technicians every year. It will, therefore, be necessary, especially with a view to increasing the force of subordinate technicians, *to build up on a wide scale the system of technical evening schools for workingmen,* or of other equivalent training courses. In this manner a new corps of foremen and overseers will be recruited from among the most advanced and most intelligent workers in industry. To attain this object, the present system of workers' evening schools, with an aggregate attendance of 10,000 and with only 1,500 graduates a year, is obviously inadequate. The adoption of the seven-hour day opens up enormous possibilities in regard to advanced training and promotion of skilled workers.

In 1927-28 the number of workers in industries controlled by the Supreme Economic Council was 2,103,000, of which 41.3 per cent were classed as skilled and 58.7 per cent as unskilled workers. It is believed by some that the character of the technical reconstruction of industry provided in the five-year plan does not require any further increase in the relative importance of skilled workers in relation to the total. Such a notion is hardly correct when stated in this categorical form. But irrespective of the merits of this disputed point there is one thing *not open to question, and that is the necessity of raising the whole mass of skilled labor to a higher technical level, and, of course, to a higher cultural level,* in order that the workers may be able to adapt them-

NUMBER OF STUDENTS AND GRADUATES
(in thousands)

	1927-28	*1928-29*	*1929-30*	*1930-31*	*1931-32*	*1932-33*	*Total Number of Graduates for Five Years*
Factory training of apprentices:							
students	89.3	105.9	169.2	186.9	205.2	224.8	....
graduates ..	....	27.0	33.4	40.0	53.1	62.8	216.3
Central Institute of Labor:							
students	....	11.6	17.0	24.9	27.4	33.6	....
graduates ..	....	11.5	16.9	24.7	26.9	32.5	112.5
Vocational schools:							
students	31.0	33.8	36.4	38.9	41.3	45.1	....
graduates ..	....	5.6	5.6	6.8	10.7	15.9	44.6
Continuation courses for workers:							
students	41.5	70.0	528.2	675.8	728.2	812.0	....
graduates ..	....	68.2	211.4	269.0	289.7	329.1	1167.4

selves to the new equipment and the new system of production which will result from the investment of 13 billion rubles in industry regulated by the Supreme Economic Council. In fact, at the present time there is already *keenly felt a growing contradiction between the efficiency of the new equipment and the low technical culture of the worker attending it.* For this reason the program provides for ***the proper training and retraining*** of a minimum of 1.3 million workers.

The table on page 118 shows the contributions of the various types of Soviet technical schools in supplying skilled workers for industry, as estimated by the five-year plan.

In all, the number of skilled workers to be graduated from trade schools in the five years will amount to 1,540,800. At the end of the five-year period there will be 2,806,000 workers in the industries regulated by the Supreme Economic Council, of whom about 55 per cent will be skilled. The total outlays for the training and retraining of skilled workers provided for the five years will amount to about *one billion rubles.* Here, however, money is not what matters most; the promise of success lies in a new organization of this extremely important field.

2. SKILLED PERSONNEL IN CONSTRUCTION WORK

In discussing the problem of the training of skilled workers, special place should be given to the most backward field in this respect, which is that of construction. The great tasks set for the five years in regard to the rationalization of construction work and reduction of costs require that attention be paid not only to the new construction machinery and mechanical devices to be introduced, but also to the human labor engaged in the process. According to present estimates, the number of skilled workers that will be required in construction during the period is about 230,000. The specific characteristics of construction workers as a group and the seasonal nature of their work make the matter of training new skilled workers and, even more so, of raising the qualifications of the old workers particularly difficult. It may be expected that the Central Institute of Labor will train about 95,000 persons during the five years, the continuation schools for workers up to 112,000, and that about 17,000 workers will be trained through the special building courses for apprentices (Stroyuch). The total cost of these measures is estimated at about 55,000,000 rubles.

3. SKILLED PERSONNEL IN TRANSPORTATION

A feature of the development program in transportation that distinguishes it from the similar programs in other economic fields, is that the 85 per cent increase in the work of the railways is to be brought about mainly through reorganization, with the total number of employees remaining practically unchanged. This fact, as well as the comparatively simple distribution of skilled workers in transportation, makes it possible to estimate the future requirements of skilled personnel in this field with a fair degree of accuracy.

According to estimates made in 1928, the total number of railway posts that should be held by engineers was 9,600, of which only 3,300 were actually filled by engineers, while the remainder were held by technicians and undergraduates. In accordance with the requirements, as estimated by transportation authorities, the total number of railway engineers will have to be increased in the five years up to 6,400. The number of engineers required for water transportation at the end of the period is estimated at about 1,000, and the same number or somewhat more will be needed for local transport. Taking into consideration the number of engineers graduating from the two Institutes of Transportation in Moscow and Leningrad, the general system of higher technical schools will have to supply about 3,500 engineers for transportation.

The total number of technicians in the railway service is now about 10,000, of whom 40 per cent are classed as first grade. In accordance with the planned reconstruction, the total number of technicians will have to be increased to about 22,000 during the period, the distribution by grades remaining unchanged. The technical school system as it now exists cannot meet this demand, and it will be necessary to provide an additional number of schools for workers, special training schools, or similar organizations.

As regards, finally, the training of skilled workmen for transportation, the total number that will be required by the end of the five-year period is estimated at about 500,000, including 290,000 in train service, about 150,000 in maintenance of way service, 50,000 in signalling and communication service, and about

10,000 in all other services. There is not expected to be any noticeable change in the relative proportions of skilled and unskilled workers, and only very slight modifications in the forms of training now provided will be required. The aim will be to further rationalize the training, to enlarge the attendance of apprentices' schools, and to widen the system of courses for adult workers.

4. SKILLED PERSONNEL IN AGRICULTURE

The *question of skilled personnel in agriculture is one that calls for the most serious attention.* The five-year plan aims at a tremendous advance in agriculture as a whole and, in particular, at the development of the socialized sector, with the aid of machine technique applied on the widest scale. It implies, accordingly, an advance of the peasant masses on the road to agricultural progress, such as has hitherto not been witnessed. It is necessary, therefore, to face squarely the problem as to the corps of skilled organizers to lead this movement in its technical phase.

In 1927-28 there were in the country about 5,000 agricultural aid stations with about 9,500 agronomists of various qualifications. The number of agronomists will be increased by the end of the period to 23,000. This is a task which will heavily tax the resources of the existing higher agricultural schools. Nevertheless, it must be accomplished in full or even enlarged, if possible, but not under any circumstances be reduced. It should also be borne in mind that the transition to a wide application of machine methods and to large-scale farming *requires not only agronomists, but also large numbers of qualified engineers.* Besides, as regards the agronomists themselves, the process of mechanization will also involve higher demands upon them. The higher agricultural schools are thus confronted with the problem of adapting the character of their courses to the sweeping changes in agricultural methods.

Besides a large engineering personnel, there will also be required in agriculture an army of about *250,000 skilled workers, including some 200,000 tractor operators and 50,000 mechanics.* In view of the great tasks set in regard to the utilization of machinery and increasing the efficiency of work, considerable attention must be given to a proper training of this personnel.

Finally, there is the *separate problem of agricultural education of the peasant masses.* There is no prospect that the tasks set for agriculture will be accomplished, or that the work of the agronomists and engineers will be productive, unless a large vanguard of active workers is recruited from among the masses of poor and middle peasants, to become the moving force of rationalization in agriculture and the agents for spreading agricultural knowledge among the masses. Collective farming will embrace about 20,000,000 people, or up to 6,000,000 peasant households. Therefore, *at least 6,000,000 peasants must be enlisted in the efforts to increase their own skill and must be provided with at least an elementary agricultural education.* This is a subject which must be thoroughly studied. For the solution of this problem the proper organizational forms and an adequate organizing personnel must be secured.

These are the most important and pressing questions among the complex group of problems connected with the training of a skilled personnel. It is obvious that these problems cannot be solved without a general cultural advance of the country, without the introduction of universal education and the abolition of illiteracy, and without the growth of a genuine civic movement aiming at a rapid improvement of the cultural and technical equipment of the masses. A ramified system of teaching by correspondence, further development of the activities of such organizations as the "Techmass,"[1] adequate financial and technical provisions for this work—these are the indispensable prerequisites for a successful solution of the personnel problem and, consequently, a successful fulfillment of the whole development program.

This educational campaign, obviously, in no way does away with the necessity of *extending the contacts* between the Soviet Union and the leading representatives of science and technique in the advanced countries of the world. The five-year program assumes an ever-increasing application of foreign technical talent for

[1] Society for the Promotion of Technical Knowledge Among the Masses.

purposes of consultation, expert investigation, lecture tours and courses, or for permanent work in the Soviet Union. At the same time, the practice of systematically sending abroad Soviet engineers, technicians, agronomists, skilled workers and, eventually, more advanced peasants as well, to enable them to become familiar with the experience of the leading industrial and agricultural countries, must likewise be extended to as great an extent and as quickly as possible. The plans in regard to exports, imports, and foreign exchange will have to include every year increasing expenditures on this account, to correspond with the provisions of the present plan.

The analysis of the personnel problem, however, leads to other and deeper problems. The conditions which surround the great development program to be accomplished demand that a number of the strongest and most gifted persons among the workers and peasants be promoted within the shortest possible time to leading positions in the economic process. Both in western Europe and, especially, in America sufficient experience has by this time been accumulated in regard to *the determination of individual vocational aptitudes for the so-called promotion from the ranks.* The Soviet Union must adopt this new science and employ it in the solution of some of the great problems of economic reconstruction.

CHAPTER V

GROWTH OF THE VOLUME OF PRODUCTION AND THE PRODUCTIVITY OF NATIONAL LABOR

THE development program discussed above and the increased production capacity of the country will be the basis of the planned increase in the volume of production and in the productivity of labor. The most important factors entering into this program have already been dealt with to some extent.

The first question that arises here is that of the rate at which industrial growth shall proceed. The five-year plan provides for an annual increase of industrial production (in industries regulated by the Supreme Council of National Economy) of from 21 to 25 per cent. It is superfluous to emphasize the tremendous importance of a yearly increase of industrial production at such a rate, and its significance as an evidence of the growth of productive forces and of the improvement in the standard of living of the people. Such a growth of industrial production in the first and most difficult stage of the reconstruction period, when many of the largest construction projects will have only been started and not yet put in operation, will be a splendid testimony of the great potentialities inherent in the organized and planned economy of the Soviet Union.

Under the five-year plan the physical volume of production (figured at 1925-26 prices) will show an increase by 1932-33, as compared with 1927-28, of 136.0 per cent in industry as a whole; in census industry [1] the increase for the five years will be 163.3 per cent and in the industries regulated by the Supreme Council of National Economy (large state industries), 179.0 per cent. Among the latter industries those in Group "A" (production of producers' goods) will show an increase in gross output of 229.5 per cent, while the industries belonging to Group "B" (production of consumers' goods) will increase their output 144.6 per cent. The *rate of growth of the total industrial output of industries manufacturing producers' goods is thus much higher than the average rate for all industries* and, of course, than for industries producing consumers' goods. This condition is a result of the accelerated process of industrialization, and is determined primarily by the expansion of such fields as the metal industry (with an output, in 1932-33, 2.5 to 3 times as large as in 1927-28), fuel production (output to increase 2.5 times), basic chemicals (output to increase six-fold), building materials (3.5 times). However, Group "B" also (production of consumers' goods) will increase its gross output almost 2½ times in the five years. This will have the effect first of alleviating, and then of completely eliminating, the goods famine, which is one of the most important objects of the plan.

[1] See Appendix III.

The output of small-scale industry will increase 50.0 per cent. This will be attained not only through an increase in the number of workers engaged in small industries, but also through gains in the productivity of labor. The five-year plan provides for the reorganization of small establishments on a cooperative basis and for the supplying of these cooperatives with a considerable number of motors, machine tools and, in general, whatever equipment is released by the large plants in the process of reconstruction. The development of electrification will also open to small industry the possibility, at least to some extent, of being included among the consumers of electric power. Without interfering in any way with the triumphant advance of big industry, these provisions will result in a combination of large and small industry, which will open up considerable opportunities for numerous groups of artisans and handicraftsmen in the coming period. It is sufficient to mention that the plan provides for an addition of 900,000 workers to the number now engaged in small trades. It is obvious that this will have great significance in reducing unemployment, which will still remain one of the adverse aspects of Soviet life in the period under consideration.

In the discussion of the general development program were indicated the production tasks assigned to the several leading industries. By the end of the five-year period, *the production of electric power will reach 22 billion kilowatt-hours a year; coal production—75 mil-*

lion tons; oil production—22 million tons; pig iron—10 million tons; chemical fertilizers—7 million tons. These are the outstanding industrial goals of the five-year plan. They determine to a great extent the nature of the plan as a whole, and to their realization all other elements of the plan are more or less subordinated. The great difficulties in the way of attaining these objectives must be frankly faced. They are strongholds which will literally have to be taken by assault. It is apparent that the soundness and solidity of this production program will, in the first instance, be determined by the progress of the construction work backing up each one of these figures.

As stated above, *the output of light industry will be increased 2.4 times* in the five years, in order to mitigate and, eventually, to do away with the goods famine in the course of the period. To attain this end, there will be invested in the five years up to 3 billion rubles for the development of light industries. However, just as at the present time, the growth of the production of articles of general consumption all through the five-year period will depend primarily upon the condition of the domestic supply of raw materials and upon the possibilities of importing them. The growth of light industries as planned is conditioned upon increasing domestic cotton production to 1,907,000 tons annually, wool—to 2,200,000 tons, sugar beet—to 20,000,000 tons, etc. That is why the plan, in the endeavor to carry out the program for light industry, dwells particularly upon the necessity of assuring the supply of raw materials in the planned amounts. The fulfillment of this task will considerably lessen the dependence of light industries, by the end of the five-year period, on imported raw materials and, consequently, the dependence of domestic production of consumption goods on fluctuations of prices of raw materials in the world market. At the same time, it will permit the freeing of large foreign exchange resources for the direct needs of industrialization.

These are the objectives in regard to the physical volume of industrial production. They must be accompanied, of course, by a steady improvement in the quality of the industrial process. But that is not all. The indicated increase in output of state-owned industries must be attained *with an increase of only 33 per cent in the number of workers employed,* combined with an increase of 110 per cent in the average production per worker and a gain of 70.5 per cent in real wages. At the same time, with the aid of industrial reconstruction, the rate of fuel consumption in relation to output will be reduced 30 per cent on the average, the consumption of agricultural raw materials per unit of output—18 per cent and that of industrial raw materials—28 per cent. These factors, together with all other technical improvements, will mean a *35 per cent reduction in the costs of industrial production.*

This is an element of decisive importance, not only for industry, but for the five-year plan as a whole.

In the very first year of the period covered by the plan, the reduction of industrial costs has become the central problem of the economic plan and of all economic activity. The struggle for lowered costs bulks as the centre of attention for the industrial personnel as well as for the general Soviet public. Cost reduction has been defined as "the central problem of industry, to the solution of which all other problems must be subordinated." The five-year plan accordingly places that problem at the head of all efforts of reconstruction and rationalization. In individual industries and in particular stages the necessity of increasing the volume of production at an accelerated pace may possibly come into conflict with cost reduction. But the general trend of industrial reconstruction must intimately combine a large quantitative growth of production with the maximum lowering of costs. Without this, successful economic competition with more advanced countries will be unthinkable; it will be impossible to assure the flow of capital investments at the planned rate; there will be no possibility for industry to fulfill its historical mission of leading the way towards a radical reconstruction of agriculture.

The tasks that confront Soviet industry in the five-year period now setting in are thus extremely formidable, not only in regard to development work (which was discussed above) but also in regard to operating problems. The Soviet Union cannot curtail production or close down industrial plants during their reconstruction. A distinguishing feature of the plan, and one that constitutes its greatest difficulty, is that *reconstruction and new construction on a large scale must be carried on in industry, while production is maintained at the highest level.* This is an indispensable condition if industry is to accomplish its part as a factor in the steady economic growth of the country, unhampered by crises.

In regard to *agricultural production,* the tasks set by the five-year plan are not any smaller in scope, and the conditions under which they will have to be carried out are even more difficult. The prevalence of small-scale farming with its dependence upon uncontrollable natural factors, and a number of unfavorable circumstances which developed at the beginning of the five-year period, give the estimates of agricultural production for the coming five years a rather conditional character. That is why this field, in particular, demands the concentration of all available methods and resources for the stimulation of production.

The production program in agriculture provides for a total *increase of the area planted* to all crops of about 22.8 per cent by the spring of 1932 and 26.4 per cent by the spring of 1933; the grain acreage will be increased 15.2 per cent, and that sown to industrial crops, 64.4 per cent. Inasmuch as the grain area is still lower than before the war, and in view of the high rate of the growth of population and the rapid industrial development, this extension of the acreage *must be regarded as a minimum,* which cannot be reduced under any circumstances. The difficulties in regard to food supply with which the country has had to contend at the outset of the five-year period are in themselves a sufficient argument for a large extension of the area under cultivation. As stated above, the additional grain area will constitute about 15 million hectares, located chiefly in the Volga region and in the Eastern regions of the country, that is, primarily in areas of extensive farming. Of the greatest importance as an aid to this expansion will be the mechanization of agriculture and, especially, the introduction of tractors.

Next in order but of decisive importance as a factor in the increase of agricultural production, will be *the struggle for higher crop yields.* During the remaining four years of the period under consideration the five-year plan provides for an increase of about 25 per cent in the yield per acre of grain, a 34 per cent increase for cotton and 57 per cent for flax.

The anticipated growth of agricultural output is determined by the combination of these two factors of acreage extension and higher yields, both of which must be utilized to the maximum degree. The essential figures relating to this growth of production are shown in the table on the following page.

This rate of growth of agricultural production and, in particular, of grain production, will not only afford a solution of the problem of domestic food supply and permit the accumulation of grain reserves, but *will also, beginning with the third year of the period under con-*

sideration, permit the resumption of grain exports from the Soviet Union in fairly large quantities. With an increase in gross production from 73.7 million metric tons in 1927-28 to 100 million tons in 1932-33, the estimates of the grain balance anticipate an accumulation of stocks in the five years to the amount of 4.9 million tons, about 2.2 million tons being accumulated as early as 1930-31. After allowing for the increase

AGRICULTURAL PRODUCTION
(In Billions of Rubles at 1926-27 Prices)

	1927-28	*1932-33*	*Ratio of 1932-33 to 1927-28 Per Cent*
Total agricultural output	14.5	22.6	155.9
Including:			
(a) Plant cultures (total)	9.2	14.5	157.6
Of which, grain	3.7	5.6	151.4
industrial crops .	0.91	1.85	203.2
(b) Animal products, ...	4.8	7.1	147.9
Of which, raw materials ...	0.65	0.80	123.1
foodstuffs	4.12	6.36	154.4

in stocks, as well as for increased rate of food consumption, seeds and animal feed, there should be available for export in the last year of the period about 8 million tons.

The growth of production of industrial crops anticipated by the plan is predicated on the use of chemical fertilizers on almost 100 per cent of the cultivated area, with a resulting increase in crop yields, and on the increase in acreage indicated above. The gains in production during the period of the most important crops of this group may be seen in the following table (in millions of metric tons):

	1927-28	*1932-33*	*Ratio of 1932-33 to 1927-28 Per Cent*
Oil seed	3.40	6.72	197.6
Cotton, unginned	.72	1.91	265.3
Flax, fiber	.29	.62	213.9
Sugar beets	10.10	19.55	193.6

The carrying out of this program will fully guarantee the growth of production planned for light industry, and will greatly lessen its dependence upon foreign raw materials.

The output of animal products, according to the plan, will increase by almost 50 per cent, which presupposes a considerable increase in the number of live stock and an improvement in its quality in every animal-raising region. This will constitute one of the most important phases of agricultural reconstruction. Carried out to its furthest development, the growth of animal raising along new lines, together with the progress of industrialization, will eventually lead to a basic transformation of that structure of agriculture which was characteristic of the pre-revolutionary period.

In the preceding discussion we have repeatedly emphasized the tremendous growth of the socialized sector in agriculture, which is the most important feature of the program of agricultural development. The following table shows the most essential changes in the relative importance of the private and socialized sectors to be brought about during the five-year period (in percentages of the total):

	Years	Private Sector	Socialized Sector: Total	Socialized Sector: State Farms	Socialized Sector: Cooperative and Collective Farms
		Per Cent			
(1) Area under cultivation (total)	1927-28	98.0	2.0	1.1	0.9
	1932-33	81.9	18.1	3.5	14.6
Including grain acreage	1927-28	98.0	2.0	1.1	0.9
	1932-33	83.6	16.4	3.3	13.1
(2) Gross grain production	1927-28	97.9	2.1	1.1	1.0
	1932-33	80.2	19.8	4.5	15.3
(3) Marketable portion of grain production	1927-28	92.5	7.5	3.7	3.8
	1932-33	57.4	42.6	17.3	25.3
(4) Total gross agricultural production	1927-28	98.2	1.8	1.2	0.6
	1932-33	85.3	14.7	3.2	11.5
(5) Marketable portion of total agricultural production	1927-28	95.6	4.4	3.6	0.8
	1932-33	74.7	25.3	8.6	16.7

This table requires no commentary. The enormous tasks set for the socialized sector, in regard both to volume of production and to improvement in methods, arise from the fact that the five-year period covered by the plan will inaugurate the process of rapid socialization in agriculture. The fate of this tremendous historical transformation will depend largely on the suc-

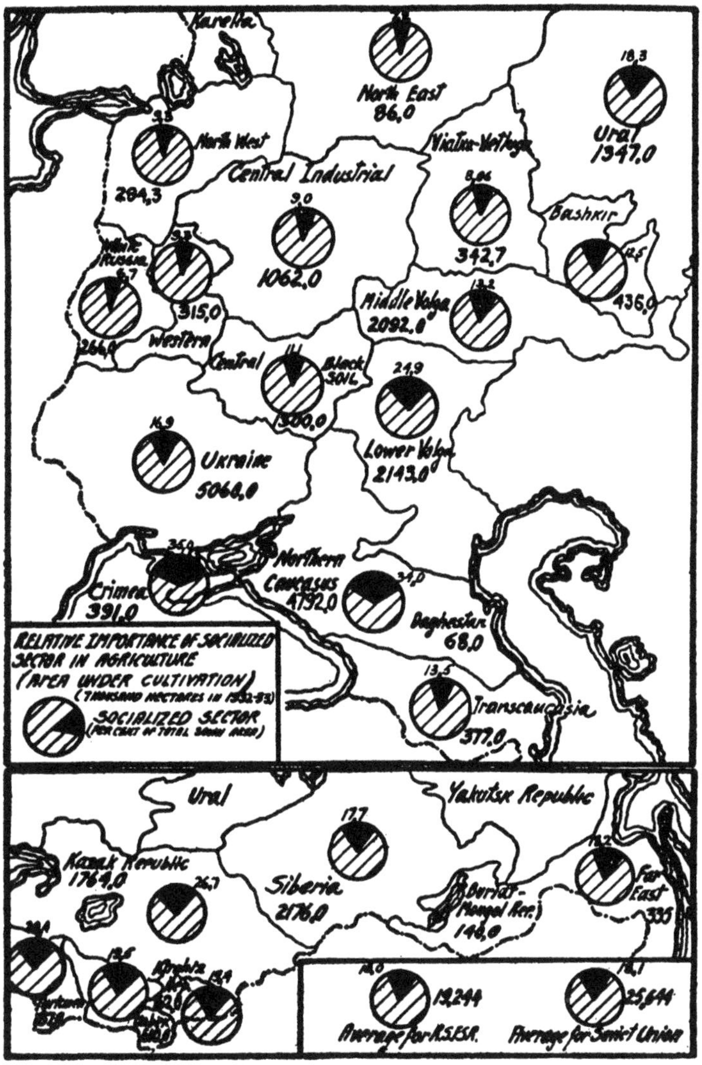
Karelia
North East
86,0
18,3
Ural
1347,0
9,5
North West
284,3
Central Industrial
9,0
1062,0
Viatka-Vetluga
8,66
342,7
Bashkir
12,5
436,0
White Russia
5,7
264,0
315,0
Western
Middle Volga
2092,0
13,2
Central
Black SOIL
3300,0
24,9
Lower Volga
2143,0
16,9
Ukraine
5068,0
36,0
Crimea
391,0
Northern Caucasus
4792,0
34,0
Daghestan
68,0
13,5
Transcaucasia
377,0
RELATIVE IMPORTANCE OF SOCIALIZED SECTOR IN AGRICULTURE
(AREA UNDER CULTIVATION)
(THOUSAND HECTARES IN 1932-33)
SOCIALIZED SECTOR
(PER CENT OF TOTAL SOWN AREA)
Ural
Yakutsk Republic
17,7
Siberia
2176,0
Kazak Republic
1764,0
26,7
Buriat-Mongol Rep.
148,0
Far East
335
19,244
Average for R.S.F.S.R.
18,1
25,644
Average for Soviet Union

cess achieved in the socialized sector during the period.

The private sector, however, will still maintain its position as the mainstay of agricultural production, as it will supply, by the end of the five-year period, no less than 75 per cent of the marketable portion of the total output, even if the socialization program is fully carried out. The problems of food supply, of agricultural exports, of raw materials for industry, will depend for a solution upon the forces of the masses of poor and middle peasants with individual holdings. The five-year plan, therefore, gives the greatest attention to stimulating the production of private farms.

In this connection, the first question to come under consideration is the *price policy for agricultural products*. While industrial prices will be greatly reduced under the five-year plan, the reduction in retail prices of articles generally consumed by peasants amounting to as much as 23 per cent, the plan provides for a reduction in the general level of agricultural prices of only 5.4 per cent by 1932-33 as compared with 1927-28; prices of grain will be reduced 5.2 per cent, industrial crops—9.6 per cent and animal products—7.6 per cent.

Another means of stimulating individual peasant farms to greater production will be through the medium of the *agricultural tax*. The provisions of the plan in this respect conform with the measures enacted by the government for the year 1928-29, which inaugurated the taxation policy to be followed in the subsequent years. The anticipated returns from the agricultural tax are as follows (in millions of rubles):

1927-28	349
1928-29	400
1929-30	375
1930-31	405
1931-32	435
1932-33	600
Total for five years, 1928-29 to 1932-33	2,215

This taxation policy, especially in the first years of the period, will serve as an incentive to the whole mass of middle peasants to increase their acreage, to apply better methods of farming and, in general, to exert their efforts toward an increase of production. This is one of the most essential points for the entire economic plan.

A further factor contributing to the same result is the *process of extending the system of cooperatives among the peasantry.* By the end of the five-year period up to 85 per cent of all peasant households will be embraced by cooperative organizations. Agricultural cooperation figures in the five-year plan as a powerful organizer and promoter of production and an important factor in the advance of agriculture to the level required by the industrialization program of the country. The method of contracting of grain crops, which will be steadily extended on an ever-widening scale in the course of the period, will be increasing in importance each year and will also play an important part in stimulating increased production of individual peasants.

Finally, as another economic weapon, there must be stressed the general policy in regard to the *distribution of national income and the comparative improvements in the standards of living of the agricultural and non-agricultural populations,* as provided under the plan. According to these provisions the standard of living of the two groups will improve to about the same extent. This means that an end will be put to the growth of the discrepancy between the standards of living of the city and the country. The complete elimination of this discrepancy is one of the great objects of socialism, which will be attained only in a more distant future. Nevertheless, the trend of the five-year period in this respect, which is an outcome of the policy in regard to prices, taxation, etc., will be a helpful factor in stimulating increased production by the peasant population.

In addition to the economic levers described above, the plan provides for the furthering of agricultural production through *intensive mechanization of farming, the application of chemistry, and the industrialization of agriculture in the broadest sense.* The scale on which these measures will be carried out has been described in detail in the discussion of the general development program for agriculture. The same end will be promoted by the *system of agricultural education,* a brief idea of which has likewise been given above, in the chapter on the problem of skilled personnel.

The obstacles to agricultural production noted in the first year of the period covered by the plan are such as to cause considerable concern over the success of the plan as a whole. However, *the decisive steps taken to enlist state industry in the service of agriculture* (through the program of production of agricultural machinery, supply of tractors, the production of fertilizers, etc.), *the building up of the socialized sector in agriculture, the various economic measures designed to stimulate individual peasant production, and the program regarding the training of skilled workers for agriculture*—all these warrant the expectation that the resistance of the minority of exploiters among the peasants will be broken and that the great mass of the poor and middle peasants will be firmly established on the road to agricultural progress.

The *production program in transportation* provides for an 85 per cent increase in freight traffic. Above has been described in detail the plan of reconstruction and of new construction which will enable the transportation system to carry out this program. A special feature of the five-year plan for transportation is the fact that the great expansion in operations will have to be accomplished with almost no increase in personnel. This bespeaks, primarily, the extent and the thoroughness of the program of railway reconstruction. The reduction of transportation costs is set at more than 20 per cent.

Such are the most essential facts relating to the

growth of the volume of production and of the productivity of national labor under the five-year plan. These production tasks are no less difficult or responsible than those of the general development plan, with which they are most intimately connected. Current production must be maintained on a high and ever-rising level. And if the five-year development program is a mighty test for the technical and organizing personnel of the country, the program in the field of current production is just as tremendous a test for the working masses as a whole.

CHAPTER VI

THE PROBLEM OF LABOR

One of the most urgent problems to be faced in the five-year period covered by the plan is that of the labor resources of the country and their utilization. The natural growth of the population in the Soviet Union is proceeding at a rate unknown in any other Western country. The annual rate of natural population increase is 1.3 per 1,000 in France, 7.9 in Germany, 6.4 in England, 10.3 in Italy, 23.0 per 1,000 in the U.S.S.R. With a population of over 150,000,000, the annual increase in the Soviet Union is at least 3.5 millions, whereas all the countries of Western Europe combined, with an aggregate population of 370,000,000, show a growth of only 2.5 million souls a year. In five years the total increase in population in the Soviet Union will be 18,000,000 and in the population of working age, over 9,000,000. At the same time, as the result of the process of industrialization, there is taking place an *impetuous growth of cities, which is likewise outstripping the rate of this movement in foreign countries or in pre-war Russia.* Whereas in Germany, England and the United States, the annual rate of growth of the urban population in the period from 1900 to 1905 never exceeded 3.3 per cent, and only the United

States was able to attain that rate in the period from 1900 to 1910, in the Soviet Union the urban population increased 5.5 per cent in 1926 and 5.0 per cent in 1927.

This relatively rapid growth of the urban population is doubtless to be accounted for by the fact that, whereas in other countries the rationalization of industry brings with it a relative and also sometimes an absolute decrease in the number of workers, economic reconstruction in the Soviet Union has been accompanied by an increase in the number, due to the expansion of production and the reduction of working hours. This tremendously important factor will manifest itself very clearly in the period under consideration. Notwithstanding the great achievements expected in the process of rationalization of production, the number of workers will be steadily increasing, although at a much slower rate than in the preceding period. At the same time, the rapid increase in urban population is also influenced by agrarian overpopulation, a phenomenon inherited from the pre-revolutionary period. The economic policy of the Soviet government (promotion of agriculture, development of collective methods of farming, improvement in the standard of living of the poor peasant groups, etc.) is leading to a gradual elimination of this condition of agrarian overpopulation. However, in the coming period it will still have to be faced as an indisputable fact. The number of persons expected to migrate from rural to urban communities in the course of the five years is estimated at about 2.5 or 3 millions. It will be the task of the Soviet economic system to enroll these forces in the ranks of socially useful labor.

In the work on the five-year plan an attempt was made to arrive at an *estimate of the movement of labor* for the five years. While these estimates are subject to limitations they, nevertheless, afford the possibility of forming a judgment in regard to changes in the unutilized balance of labor resources and of thus answering the question as to what extent the sum total of measures designed to increase the productive forces of the country will solve the problem of alleviating unemployment. According to those estimates, *the number of unemployed will be reduced from 1.1 millions in 1927-28 to 400,000 in 1932-33,* which may be regarded as almost the normal amount of unemployment technically unavoidable in the regular course of economic life, including as it does unemployment resulting from labor turnover, etc.

The plan also shows a fairly satisfactory condition in regard to the economic position of adolescents and of young people in cities by the end of the five-year period. The number of adolescents (16 to 18 years of age) in cities is estimated to amount to 1.3 millions by that time, of whom about 900,000 will be attending schools and 400,000 engaged in production (at the present time over 500,000 persons in this age group are working). Young people between the ages of 18 to 24 in cities will number 4.6 millions, of whom about 400,-

000 will be in schools and the remainder in production.

These favorable tendencies in regard to unemployment must not, of course, be permitted to bring about any curtailment whatsoever in the aid extended to unemployed or any reduction in appropriations for this purpose. On the contrary, the plan provides further increases of these allotments.

I. NUMBER OF WAGE EARNERS

The growth of the total number of wage earners in the five years is estimated as follows in the plan (in thousands):

	1927-28	*1932-33*	*Ratio of 1932-33 to 1927-28 Per Cent*
Total number of persons working for hire	11,350	15,764	138.9
Total, exclusive of workers in agriculture and in forestry	9,226	12,897	139.8

Thus, the total number of wage earners will increase 38.9 per cent in the five years, while for the non-agricultural proletariat the increase will be even larger, namely, 39.8 per cent.

In comparison with the preceding five-year period, which showed an annual increase of 11 to 12 per cent in the total number of wage earners, these estimates appear small. It should be observed, however, that in the years of economic rehabilitation the growth of hired labor was mainly a result of the gradually increasing utilization of the *basic capital already available,* with a comparatively insignificant expansion of basic capital. On the other hand, the growth of production in the five-year period covered by the present plan will come about primarily through a tremendous expansion of productive capacity, effected through *radical reconstruction of old plants and construction of new enterprises.* With the transition from the period of rehabilitation to that of new development, the increase in labor employed per unit of basic capital will inevitably proceed at a slower rate. It may be noted, however, that the number of workers in the construction field will show an increase of over 200 per cent in the five years.

In transportation the requirements of additional workers will, likewise, arise chiefly in connection with new railway construction.

An examination of the changes in the number of workers from year to year shows that the rate of increase in 1929-30 is somewhat greater than in the preceding year, and that the rate of increase gradually slows down in the succeeding years. The average annual increase in the number of workers for the five-year period as a whole is 6 per cent. The significance of this rate of increase is clearly brought out when it is compared with the rate of growth of the working force and the general population of pre-war days. Only in the very infancy of capitalism in Russia did the growth of the proletariat exceed that estimated in the present plan. Even in the years of industrial prosperity preceding the war, leaving out of consideration periods of depression, the number of workers increased at the rate of not over 3 or 4 per cent a year.

In 1927-28 the number of persons working for hire in the Soviet Union was 11.4 millions, or 13.8 per cent of the total population of working age (82.4 millions). By the end of the five-year period under consideration the corresponding proportion will be 17 per cent. In other words, *the relative importance of the proletariat will increase* by almost 25 per cent in the five years. Thus the improvements in technique and in organization to be brought about will be accompanied by a considerable increase, not only absolute but relative as well, in the labor force employed. Inasmuch as conditions in agriculture will be considerably above the pre-war level, this great absolute and relative increase in the number of wage earners will necessarily mean reduced unemployment, as has been pointed out above.

It is unnecessary to emphasize the enormous significance of this growth of the proletariat in relation to the total population of the Soviet Union. The process of socialist industrialization and rationalization is bound to be closely linked up with the increased importance of the rôle of the proletariat.

2. PRODUCTIVITY OF LABOR AND WAGES

The outstanding phase of economic development in the plans for the five-year period, is the radical reconstruction of the power situation and the increase in mechanical aids to human labor. As shown above, the consumption of mechanical and electric energy in industry in 1932-33 will amount to 2.61 kilowatt-hours per man-hour, as against 1.24 kilowatt-hours in 1927-28—in other words, twice as large. In transportation, the increase in the same period will be from 2.05 kilowatt-hours to 3.11 kilowatt-hours, or 51.7 per cent. In agriculture the available capacity of animal and mechanical power per worker will increase 20.7 per cent. The increase in the socialized sector of agriculture will be many times greater—184 per cent on state farms (from 475 to 1,350 kilowatts), and 124 per cent on collective farms (from 175 to 390 kilowatts), whereas in the private sector the increase will amount to only about 13 per cent.

Relying chiefly on this factor, the productivity of labor will increase 110 per cent in industry, 60 per cent in construction, and 75 per cent in transportation. At this stage of the work it has so far been impossible to prepare an estimate of the growth of productivity in agriculture. The increased use of mechanical power, however, is only one of the factors in the increase of productivity of labor. Along with it, there will be working with undiminished significance during the period still another factor, namely, the increasing intensity of labor. It is, of course, impossible to give a numerical expression to the separate effect of either factor. The increase of productivity in the principal industries under the combined action of both factors will be about as follows:

INDUSTRIES

Group "A" *(Producers' Goods)*	*Increase in Five Years* *Per Cent*
(1) Fuel	100
(2) Metal mining	100
(3) Metal manufacturing	130
(4) Electrical equipment	136
(5) Building materials	110
(6) Lumber and woodworking	103
(7) Chemical	84
Group "B" *(Consumers' Goods)*	
(1) Textile	97
(2) Needle trades	170
(3) Leather and shoe	96
(4) China and porcelain	68
(5) Chemical	120
(6) Food and allied industries	104
(7) Salt	35
(8) Paper	128

Average increase for all industries 110 per cent.

Along with the expanding of the forces of the industrial proletariat goes the very important problem of *guaranteeing the growth of real wages.* The rise of real wages is closely interwoven with the problem of increasing the share of the proletariat in the national income, of stimulating the productivity of labor in every possible way, of the ability of the market to meet the increase in wages, and of the accumulation of capital in the socialized sector of national economy.

As far as the relation between wages and productivity of labor is concerned, the object to be attained in the period of reconstruction, and especially in its initial stage, is an *increase in the productivity of labor at a faster rate than that of the increase of wages.* However, the difference between these rates should be made less as the relative importance of the intensity of labor in increased productivity becomes greater, and more when the gain in productivity appears rather as the result of technical improvements. At the same time, of course, the general Soviet policy of advancing wages in the lowest paid industries will be maintained.

The plan provides for an increase in money wages in industry as a whole of 47 per cent in five years. To some extent this increase reflects the rise of the relative importance of salaried employees (technical personnel), who are paid at a rate much above the average for all employees.

In the first years of the New Economic Policy the conditions under which the restoration of industry was proceeding were such as to permit wages to be increased much faster in light industries than in the heavy branches. This was due to the fact that the former group were working for a broader market, and also to the comparatively small relative weight of wages in the total production costs. On the other hand, in the industries which produce producers' goods, and especially in the coal and metal industries, wage increases were made difficult by the necessity of intensively developing these industries and, also, by the high relative importance of the wage item in their total costs. To correct this situation and to establish wage rates in the various industries corresponding with the qualifications of the workers is the aim of the five-year plan in charting the wages for the several branches of industry. According to preliminary estimates the relative wage levels in the different industries is as follows:

Classes of Workers	*1913*	*1927-28*	*1932-33*	*Ratio of average wage in 1932-33 to 1927-28*
	Per Cent of Average Wage			*Per Cent*
(1) Metal workers	140.0	120.4	125.8	153.8
(2) Miners	132.0	92.1	100.3	159.9
(3) Wood workers	88.0	94.0	87.7	137.0
(4) Paper workers	72.0	92.4	87.6	139.3
(5) Printers	128.0	135.0	119.0	129.5
(6) Textile workers	68.0	83.4	81.2	143.4
(7) Leather workers	100.0	129.3	110.3	125.3
(8) Food workers	80.0	118.5	102.8	127.4
(9) Chemical workers ...	80.0	100.7	92.5	135.0
All industries combined	100.0	100.0	100.0	146.9

Taking into account the reduction in the cost of living expected and the various social insurance benefits received by workers and their dependents, real wages of industrial workers will increase 70.5 per cent by 1932-33 as compared with 1927-28, and 108.9 per cent as compared with 1913.

The most important changes provided in regard to wages are those affecting metal workers and miners (chiefly in coal mining).

The above estimates must be thoroughly reworked and revised in order to make them conform more fully with labor conditions in the several industries. Miners' wages, in particular, should be still further increased. It should be noted that the plan does not at all aim to restore the relationship between wages in industries existing prior to the war, as the conditions then prevailing cannot in any degree serve as a model for the Soviet Union.

In transportation and communication the increase in money wages provided in the plan will be about 39 per cent. If account is taken of the changes to be effected in the relative numbers of various classes of workers in transportation, this *increase is practically identical with the growth of wages of industrial workers,* and it has so been designed by the plan. Wages of railway workers will increase somewhat faster than the average for all workers in transportation.

In *construction* the increase in wages will be about 30 per cent, as it has been considered necessary to bring closer together the wages of industrial and construction workers.

Finally, the highest rate of increase has been provided in the remuneration of workers in *social and cultural service, namely, about 72 per cent for educational workers and about 47 per cent for those in the public health service.* Even these increases, however, will not result in equalizing the status of these groups with that of industrial workers, in regard to the absolute amount of remuneration in the five-year period. In 1932-33, the earnings of workers in this class will amount to about 90 per cent of the average earnings of industrial workers, as against 75 per cent in 1927-28.

The pay of workers in *general administrative services* will be increased 35 per cent, particular attention being given to the improvement of the condition of the rank and file of Soviet employees.

These changes will mean, for all classes of workers combined, an average increase in wages of about 38 per cent, or of 48 per cent, if the socialized portion of wages is included. Inasmuch as a 14 per cent reduction in the cost of living is anticipated, *real (individual) wages will increase about 66 per cent.*

Mention has just been made of the *socialized portion of wages.* In mapping out the movement of real wages in the five-year period, it has been considered necessary to provide that a certain portion of the wages be socialized, primarily for the purpose of improving the education of workers' children, that is, for increasing, in an organized manner, that part of the workers' budget which goes for cultural needs. If only a very small portion of the wage increase in the remaining four years of the period under consideration is socialized, it will be possible to set up a fund of over one billion rubles, which will be of enormous aid in connection with the problem of the education of proletarian children—a matter of deep interest and concern for the working masses.

3. LENGTH OF WORKING DAY

In conformity with the directives contained in the historical manifesto of the Central Executive Committee of the Soviet Union, the plan provides for a *general introduction of the seven-hour day* in all industrial establishments of the country. The average normal working day will be reduced from 7.71 hours in 1927-28 to 6.86 hours in 1932-33, or by 11 per cent in the five years. *As compared with pre-revolutionary conditions, the working day in industry is now, on the average, 2.18 hours shorter, and in 1932-33 it will be shorter by 3.03 hours.*

Taking into account the shorter hours on Saturdays and on days before holidays, the working week will be reduced from 44.6 hours in 1927-28 to 40.2 hours at the end of the five-year period. This reduction in working hours, together with the provisions for increasing the number of proletarians and for advancing wages, are among those points which embody most completely the general principles underlying the economic plan of the Soviet Union. Whereas, in most other countries the process of rationalization of industry since the war has meant fewer workers, longer hours, and lower wages, socialist rationalization, as carried out in the Soviet Union, is accompanied from the very first stages, that is, from the most difficult ones, by an increase in the number of workers, a considerable rise in real wages, and a substantial reduction of working hours. If the growth of productive forces in the Soviet Union proceeds in accordance with the plan, it will be perfectly possible *by the end of the five-year period to raise the question of further reducing the working day,* that is, of gradually introducing the six-hour day.

4. SOCIAL INSURANCE AND LABOR PROTECTION

Social insurance benefits will likewise be greatly extended under the provisions of the five-year plan. Unlike other countries, the Soviet Union places the cost of social insurance in its entirety upon the employing establishments, thus making it a direct addition to wages.

The social insurance budget will increase from 969 million rubles in 1927-28 to 1,950 million rubles in 1932-33, that is by more than 100 per cent. This increase will result, on the one hand, from the growth in the number of employees and of their wages and, on the other, from extensions and improvements in the social insurance benefits.

Of the measures planned in the field of social insurance the most important is the provision for *old age insurance,* which by 1932-33 will extend to all classes of people working for hire. This will prove of considerable importance in helping to reduce the average age of the working force.

The estimated changes in the volume and in the distribution of the social insurance budget may be seen from the following table (in millions of rubles):

	1927-28	*1932-33*	*Ratio of 1932-33 to 1927-28 Per Cent*	*Per Cent of Total 1927-28*	*Per Cent of Total 1932-33*
Temporary disability benefits	239.7	452.1	189	24.8	23.2
Special benefits (childbirth, burial, etc.)	69.8	92.2	132	7.2	4.7
Permanent disability benefits	203.8	527.4	259	21.0	27.1
Old age benefits	....	56.6	....	....	2.9
Unemployment benefits	112.7	217.0	193	11.6	11.1
Houses of rest and sanatoria	35.8	60.6	169	3.7	3.1
Medical assistance	240.6	419.7	174	24.8	21.5
Other expenses and reserve funds	66.8	124.7	187	6.9	6.4
Total	969.2	1950.3	201	100.0	100.0

Appropriations for the protection of health and safety of the workers in large-scale state industries will amount for the five-year period to about 320 million rubles. In addition to these direct provisions, an even more considerable improvement, in regard to the reduction of accidents and to the protection of the health of workers in industry, will result from the general reconstruction of industry, the greater power equipment and, consequently, the substitution of mechanical energy for muscular work, the introduction of new machines and appliances, the enlargement of working premises, better layout of equipment, etc.

CHAPTER VII

EQUILIBRIUM OF SUPPLY AND DEMAND, CONSUMPTION, AND PRICE POLICY

THE five-year economic plan, in its every aspect, starts from the general directions of the government in regard to the necessity of relieving the goods famine in the immediate future, and of terminating it entirely before the expiration of the five-year period. This end will be attained, in the first place, through a vigorous expansion of industrial production, which has been discussed above. To guarantee with certainty, however, the attainment of this goal, it is indispensable that all factors of economic policy, such as prices, the rate of growth of the money income of the people, taxes, loans, etc., shall also be considered in relation to the market equilibrium. It is a matter of common understanding that all calculations in regard to this question are extremely complicated and subject to qualification. The figures that will be given below must, therefore, be regarded mainly as illustrations of the general trend of the developments planned.

According to estimates made in connection with the five-year plan, the amount expended by workers' families for the purchase of agricultural products will decrease from about 43 per cent of their total outlay in 1927-28 to about 39.0 per cent in 1932-33, and their expenditures for manufactured products—from 34.2 to 32.5 per cent. These decreases will be accompanied by an increase in the relative importance of outlays for communal services, including housing (from 8.7 to 9.5 per cent), and for social and cultural needs (from 5.3 to 8.2 per cent), while all other expenses will increase from 3.8 to 4.8 per cent of the total. Savings will increase from 5.0 per cent of the total budget of the city population to about 6.0 per cent, including investments in loans, savings deposits, shares in cooperative organizations, and cash on hand.

As regards money expenditures of the peasantry (not including dealings between peasants), disbursements for the purchases of manufactured goods will increase from 68.6 per cent of the total in 1927-28 to 71.0 per cent by the end of the five-year period, while outlays for social and cultural needs will increase from 1.2 to 3.0 per cent. Taxes will absorb 7.4 per cent of the total peasant budget in 1932-33, as against 9.7 per cent in 1927-28, and savings will increase from 4.4 to 7.8 per cent.

In comparing these urban and rural budgets, however, one should constantly bear in mind, first, the absolute sums expended for manufactured products, to which the relative increases just quoted refer. In absolute figures, these expenditures will increase in the five years for the urban population or, more precisely, for persons working for hire in cities, from 128 rubles per capita in 1927-28 to 172 rubles in 1932-33, and for the rural population, from 35 to 64 rubles per capita. It should further be noted that purchases of manufactured goods by the rural population include instruments of production. Expenses of the peasantry for this class of goods will increase 128 per cent in the five years, while outlays for articles of general consumption will increase only 41 per cent. These considerations must be kept in mind in order to get a clear understanding of the changes which the plan anticipates in the distribution of the budgets of the urban and the rural populations.

On the basis of these preliminary estimates, and with a strong emphasis on the uncertainty of calculations of this character, the movement of the demand for manufactured goods may be given about as follows (in millions of rubles):

	1927-28	*1928-29*	*1929-30*	*1930-31*	*1931-32*	*1932-33*
Demand for manufactured goods (including additions to stocks, at consumers' prices)	20,590	23,197	26,139	28,988	32,106	38,970
Balance (excess of demand—; excess of supply +)	—135	—210	—175	+75	+228	+647

The movement of the balance of supply and demand, according to the estimates of the plan, will result in a liquidation of the goods famine by the end of the five-year period. In the last three years of the period the situation in the market for manufactured goods should be well in hand, while in the year 1929-30 there will still be a considerable tension. *These favorable indications afforded by the grand totals, however, cannot be considered entirely convincing, until a thorough analysis is made of the most important markets for individual commodities of this class.* While preliminary computations have indicated that the trend in the leading individual markets will be the same as for the industrial group as a whole, additional analysis and calculations are required before a final conclusion can be drawn. The continuation of the work on this phase of the five-year plan should be based on the principle that the problem of equilibrium of supply and demand must be solved in each individual market, and it is with a view to guaranteeing this equilibrium that the work in this field must be planned.

Assuming that the program of industrial production is carried out, *the growth of the consumption* of the most important manufactured products by the population, as a whole, will be about as follows:

PER CAPITA ANNUAL CONSUMPTION

	Unit of Measurement	*1927-28*	*1932-33*
Cotton fabrics	meters	15.2	21.3
Woolen fabrics	meters	0.48	1.17
Leather footwear	pairs	0.40	0.74
Rubber shoes	pairs	0.22	0.39
Sugar	kilograms	7.7	13.9
Soap	kilograms	0.94	2.60

The program thus provides that the per capita consumption of a number of the most essential articles will be almost doubled in the half-decade.

A few words should be said in regard to the changes that will take place in the period in the distribution of manufactured goods, by sources of supply. These changes will be as follows (in per cent of total supply):

	1928-29	*1932-33*
	Per Cent	
Census industry	70.5	75.9
Small-scale industry	16.7	12.7
Imports	3.4	4.6
Other	9.4	6.8
Total	100.0	100.0

The increased importance of large-scale industry at the expense of small industries in the total supply of manufactured goods is an indirect reflection of the growth of large industrial establishments and of the concentration of production, which, in turn, are a natural outcome of the system of national economic planning. The increase in the relative importance of imported manufactures is accounted for chiefly by agricultural equipment (tractors, etc.).

The estimated changes in the relative importance of the so-called "organized" and "open" markets for manufactured goods, may be illustrated by the following figures (in percentages of total demand):

	1927-28	*1932-33*
	Per Cent	
"Organized" market	49.1	52.1
"Open" market	50.9	47.9

The share of instruments of production in the total demand of the peasant population for manufactured goods is to increase from 22.2 per cent in 1927-28 to 33.4 per cent in 1932-33.

Finally, in this connection should be mentioned the problem of stocks. According to the estimates of the plan, *all stocks* (in the hands of both producers and distributing agencies) will increase from about 20 per of the total volume of goods in 1927-28 to about 23 per cent in 1932-33; stocks held by the distribution systems will increase from 11 to 15 per cent.

These are a few factors relating to the liquidation of the shortage of manufactured goods within the five-year period. It is superfluous to add that the general problem of market equilibrium is much more intricate. It comprises, in addition, a whole series of questions connected with supplying the country with producers' goods, on the one hand, and with foodstuffs, on the other. The problem of food supply, in particular, should be emphasized here, as it has become rather acute at the outset of the five-year period under consideration, owing to a number of factors, partly of a general and partly of a specific economic nature.

The great advance in the food standards of the masses since the October revolution, and the rapid growth of cities in the process of industrialization, with the relatively slower growth of agriculture, have caused some difficulties in connection with the food supply during the years 1927-28 and 1928-29. The situation was rendered particularly acute by the disastrous winter crop of 1928 in the principal regions producing grain for the market (the Ukraine and Northern Caucasus). *The overcoming of these difficulties, the elimination of the obstacles in the way of food supply and the promotion of further improvement in the food standards of the cities and the villages, both in regard to quantity and variety*—these are among the most essential and most responsible tasks to be accomplished within the first years of the period covered by the plan. The methods of attaining these ends have been outlined in the chapter dealing with the reconstruction of agriculture, the increase of agricultural production and the reconstruction of peasant economy along socialist lines. But in this connection it is obvious that the importance of market factors, of a rational organization of exchanges between city and country, of methods of stimulating the productive efforts of the peasants through the medium of the market and, especially, of the cooperative organization of food supply in districts which depend on other regions for at least a part of their grain consumption, should not be underrated. The cooperative organizations must have a firm hold on the markets of foodstuffs in all their variety.

The per capita growth of food consumption in the five years is estimated as follows:

	Unit	*1927-28*	*1932-33*
Grain, urban population	kilograms	179	179
Grain, rural population	kilograms	221	234
Meat, urban population	kilograms	49.1	62.7
Meat, rural population	kilograms	22.6	26.4
Eggs, urban population	pieces	90.7	155.0
Eggs, rural population	pieces	49.6	72.0
Dairy products, urban population	kilograms	218.0	339.3
Dairy products, rural population	kilograms	183.0	228.0

The problems of market organization on the basis of the widest development of cooperation are among the most important phases of the five-year development plan. The capital investments required in order to provide adequate technical resources for marketing, amount to 2.2 billion rubles (at prices of the respective years). The program includes the construction of refrigerators, elevators, bread-baking plants, establishments for the preliminary treatment of agricultural raw materials, for the processing of fruit and vegetables and meat, the construction of stores, etc.

An important factor in connection with the problems of market equilibrium and likewise in regard to the social and economic objects of the plan, is the *price policy.* As has been repeatedly pointed out in the preceding discussion, the price policy laid down in the plan is designed to bring about a *systematic reduction in the general level* of prices, by means, first of all, of a contraction in industrial prices, *to attain gradually a greater equality in the exchange between city and coun-*

try, and to bring industrial prices by degrees to the level prevailing in more advanced industrial countries.

The most essential changes to be effected in the price situation in the five years may be illustrated by the following figures:

	Changes in 1932-33 as Compared with 1927-28 (increase +; decrease —) *Per Cent*
(1) Indexes of agricultural prices (producers')	
(a) General	— 5.4
(b) Grain	+ 4.8
(c) Industrial crops	— 9.6
(d) Animal products	— 7.6
(2) Retail price indexes	
(a) General	— 22.2
(b) Agricultural	— 20.6
(c) Industrial	— 22.9
(3) Index of the cost of living	
(a) General	— 14.1
(b) Items acquired in the market	— 18.0

CHAPTER VIII

THE FINANCIAL PROGRAM

In the consideration of the financial problems of the Soviet Union during the last two years, there has been noted a tendency to include much more than matters relating only to budgets and credits. An approach has been made to discussing the question of a *general plan of financing,* embracing all elements of the financial system, all the financial resources of the country. A considerable advance in this direction was made in the statistical plan for 1928-29, and the five-year plan embodies this idea even more completely. In spite of its obvious limitations, the work accomplished in this respect permits a general view to be obtained of the financial structure of the country and its basic problems in the five-year period.

The total amount of financing that will be required to carry out the five-year plan is estimated at 86 billion rubles, not including floating capital. The distribution of the sum thus to be disbursed, by general classes of expenditures, is shown in the following table (in millions of rubles):

	Amount				*Per Cent of Total*		
	1927-28	*1932-33*	*Total for Five Years 1928-29 to 1932-33*	*Ratio of 1932-33 to 1927-28 Per Cent*	*1927-28*	*1932-33*	*Five-year Period 1928-29 to 1932-33*
I. Economic Group	5,422	14,881	54,629	274.5	57.3	64.5	63.5
Including:							
(a) Industry	1,909	4,468	17,830	234.0	20.2	19.4	20.7
(b) Agriculture ..	698	1,873	6,746	268.3	7.4	8.1	7.8
(c) Electrical development ..	276	837	2,960	303.3	2.9	3.6	3.4
(d) Transportation	861	2,790	9,471	324.0	9.1	12.1	11.0
II. Social Welfare and Cultural Group	2,400	5,884	21,396	245.2	25.4	25.5	24.9
Of which: Public Education	1,029	2,995	10,385	291.1	10.9	13.0	12.1
III. General Administration and Defense	1,642	2,308	9,980	140.6	17.3	10.0	11.6
Total	9,464	23,073	86,005	243.8	100.0	100.0	100.0

The following table shows the share of the national income (in percentages of the total) which will be applied each year for the objects embraced in the general financial plan:

	Per Cent
1927-28	38
1928-29	42
1929-30	43
1930-31	45
1931-32	49
1932-33	53

In other words, by the end of the five-year period, more than a half of the total national income will be mobilized for financing under the general plan, which is a sufficient indication of the scope of the plan. The actual significance of this fact is shown even more conspicuously by the figures relating to the most important classes of expenditures under the plan. Thus, the share of the national income to be applied annually to financing the national economy, that is, exclusive of disbursements for social welfare and cultural purposes and for general government functions, will be as follows:

	Per Cent
1927-28	22
1928-29	25
1929-30	27
1930-31	28
1931-32	31
1932-33	34

At the end of the five-year period, one-third of the national income will thus pass through the machinery of the general financial system to serve for the financing of national economy and its basic reconstruction. There are many who consider that the scope of this financing is excessive. However, a thorough analysis of the program of new construction, production and financing for the five-year period, shows that such a redistribution of the national income is indispensable for a solution of the most urgent economic problems and is, at the same time, within the capabilities of the economic organism.

The distribution, by sources, of all financing under the plan is given in the table on the following page.

A notable feature of this plan is *a certain decrease in the relative importance of the budgetary sources, accompanied by an increased importance of the funds of the economic organizations themselves.* This is a direct result of the price policy outlined for the five years, which will enable industry to accumulate considerable sums, representing the difference between prices and production costs. A price policy which will bring about such a relation between prices and costs of individual products, thus permitting large savings to be effected through the mechanism of prices, is dictated by a number of considerations, such as the policy of cost reduction at a fast pace, the shortage of goods that will still prevail in the first years of the period, the great development projects, and the necessity of guaranteeing

SOURCES OF FINANCING
(In Millions of Rubles)

	Amount				Per Cent of Total		
	1927-28	*1932-33*	*Total for Five Years 1928-29 to 1932-33*	*Ratio of 1932-33 to 1927-28 Per Cent*	*1927-28*	*1932-33*	*Five-year Period from 1928-29 to 1932-33*
(1) Government budget (federal and local)	5,293	11,674	44,709	220.6	55.9	50.6	52.0
Of which:							
federal budget ..	3,514	7,547	29,639	214.8	37.1	32.7	34.5
(2) Banking system	861	1,822	6,628	211.6	9.1	7.9	7.7
(3) Social insurance	1,039	2,524	9,180	242.9	11.0	10.9	10.7
(4) Resources of economic organizations	1,680	5,201	18,961	309.6	17.8	22.5	22.0
(5) Private resources	591	1,852	6,527	313.4	6.2	8.1	7.6
Total	9,464	23,073	86,005	243.8	100.0	100.0	100.0

from the outset a rapid flow of capital investments. It should be remembered that this policy will be enforced in spite of the general reduction of industrial prices throughout the five-year period.

When the five-year plan was in preparation a much more drastic policy of price reduction was suggested. The mobilization of financial resources would, in that event, have had to be effected primarily through direct taxes and loans, that is, through the state budget and banking system. An additional argument in favor of such a policy was that direct taxes and credits are a more perfect instrument, as a matter of social principle, than the general price mechanism.

Interesting as this suggestion was, it could not, however, be adopted as the basis of the financial program. This was impossible both because of the economic situation prevailing at the outset of the five-year period and also because of the *rapid pace provided under the plan for economic development, in general, and for capital investments, in particular.* A financial policy so designed as to bring about a drastic reduction in the general price level even within the remaining years of the period under consideration, could be carried out only if the economic development of the country was being accomplished under conditions of international security. Under the existing circumstances, the financial program for the five-year period had to combine all methods of mobilizing financial resources, including accumulation through the mechanism of prices. This circumstance will necessitate, of course, a different method of handling the financial relations between industry and government than that followed in the preceding period, when the reduction in prices not only fully absorbed that of costs, but at times even exceeded it.

As may be seen from the above table, the budget, in spite of a small diminution of its relative importance as a source of financing, will still play the rôle of the chief financial weapon of the country, and will even strengthen its importance as a re-distributor of the national income. The annual share of the national income absorbed by the total combined budget (federal and local) in the preceding five-year period and the period of the plan is as follows:

	Per Cent
1923-24	16
1924-25	17
1925-26	16
1926-27	21
1927-28	24
1928-29	26
1929-30	28
1930-31	29
1931-32	30
1932-33	32

Of particular importance in financing will be the resources of the economic organizations themselves, which will furnish a total of 19 billion rubles in the five years, the social insurance funds, from which up to 9 billions will be derived, and government loans, which will yield about 6 billions during the period. This circumstance will dictate the necessity of establishing new and much stricter methods of dealing with the resources of economic organizations, of the social insurance administration, etc., which together, in the five years, will mobilize financial resources as great as those of the government budget. The financial plans of economic organizations must be drawn up and carried out with the same care and be subject to the same vigilant supervision as are now given to the government budget.

The five-year program in regard to currency issue has been designed *to guarantee a 20 per cent increase in the purchasing power of the chervonetz.* The total issue has accordingly been set at 1,250 million rubles. There is every assurance that the provisions for the five years in this regard have been made with all due caution, and that some additional reserves for financing may be found here.

The total expansion of short-term credits will amount to about 3 billion rubles, and at the same time the resources of the State Bank will increase considerably, as it will receive from the government budget about 500 million rubles in the five years, in settlement of old accounts and by direct appropriation, for the strengthening of the Bank's position.

To give a more complete idea of the financial policy embodied in the five-year plan, it will be well to cite the following figures, showing the changes in the distribution of government budgetary revenues from the various sources (in billions of rubles):

	1927-28	*1932-33*	*Total for Five Years, 1928-29 to 1932-33*	*Ratio of 1932-33 to 1927-28 Per Cent*	*Per Cent of Total 1927-28*	*Per Cent of Total 1932-33*
A. Revenues from taxation	3.3	6.7	26.3	203.0	67.9	64.5
Including:						
Direct taxes	1.5	3.6	12.6	240.0	28.4	34.4
Indirect taxes	1.7	2.9	12.9	170.6	36.9	28.0
B. Revenues from non-tax sources	0.8	2.0	7.3	250.0	17.1	19.2
C. Revenue from loans	0.7	1.7	6.0	242.9	15.0	16.5
Total (not including revenues of the People's Commissariats of Transportation and Posts and Telegraphs)	4.8	10.4	39.6	216.7	100.0	100.0

The table shows that non-tax revenues will increase at a much greater rate than those derived from taxation. The latter group, however, including indirect taxes (and also the trade and industry tax, which virtually amounts to a general tax on consumption), will also show a greatly increased yield and will continue to be the most important class of revenues.

Such a structure of the revenue side of the state budget and, in particular, the great part allotted to indirect taxes, together with the price policy laid down in the plan, will inevitably give rise to the question as to what extent this financial system as a whole is adequate, from the point of view of the class policy of the proletarian state, to what extent it is, from this same standpoint, the correct method of mobilizing financial resources for the purpose of industrial development. In replying to this question it must first of all be made clear that under the conditions of economic development in the Soviet Union, it is impossible to devise a financial system which will not require the participation of the overwhelming majority of the working population in the financing of state activities. However, the financial system embodied in the plan, even in its present imperfect form, has sufficiently powerful weapons in the shape of direct taxes (agricultural tax and income tax) to insure a strictly class character to the revenue part of the budget. But the class policy which underlies the financial system can be appraised at its full value only when the system is considered as a whole, that is, including the disbursement side of the budget. It is through the budget expenditures that the general policies of the state are carried out, in the financing of collective farm development, the extension of cooperative organization, the supplying of agricultural machinery, land organization, urban housing construction, cultural service, etc. Taken as a whole, the financial program for the five-year period will stand the test in regard to class policies just as well as in regard to all other economic criteria set up by the government.

A study of the financial program in relation to the programs of general development and capital investments, which have been discussed in preceding chapters, makes it apparent that the plan is designed to promote the task of rapidly industrializing the country. This may be clearly seen from the following figures showing the growth of that share of the budget (central and local combined) which goes annually into the financing of national economy (in percentages of total budget expenditure):

	Per Cent
1923-24	21.9
1924-25	27.9
1925-26	28.4
1926-27	38.1
1927-28	41.1
1928-29	46.1
1929-30	48.7
1930-31	50.0
1931-32	51.5
1932-33	51.0

Over one-half of the resources of the combined central and local budgets will thus be employed for economic development at the end of the five-year period, notwithstanding the fact that expenditures for cultural needs will simultaneously be showing a considerable increase, as will be shown below.

In the light of this general description of the financial

program as a whole, the financial plans relating to the various divisions of national economy may now be examined.

The *preliminary financial plan for industry* may be summarized in the following table, including floating capital (in billions of rubles):

		Total for Five Years, 1928-29 to 1932-33	*Per Cent of Total*
1. Total funds required		21.18	100.0
2. Sources of financing:	(a) Government budget	7.67	36.2
	(b) Short-term credits	1.30	6.1
	(c) Resources of industry	9.85	46.5
	(d) Other sources	2.36	11.2
Total		21.18	100.0

Here is to be noted, first of all, the great part to be played eventually by resources accumulated by the industrial organizations themselves, as a result of the discrepancy between costs and prices mentioned above. It should also be observed that, in addition to the accumulations shown in the table, an amount of about 2.4 billion rubles will be turned over from the same sources to the government budget, to be restored later by the budget to industry, in order to assure a greater concentration of industrial savings. It has been stated above that the financial relationship between industry and the state budget in the period under consideration will be different from that prevailing in the preceding five-year period. Nevertheless, under the five-year plan the budget will still show a net balance of 1.4 billion rubles to the credit of industries regulated by the Supreme Economic Council. Only under these conditions will it be possible to carry on the development work of industry on the scale and at the rate provided in the plan.

The financial plan for agriculture may be presented in a very elementary form as follows (in billions of rubles), including floating capital:

		Total for Five Years, 1928-29 to 1932-33	*Per Cent of Total*
1	Total funds required	7.88	100.0
2	Sources of financing: (a) Government budget	3.70	47.0
	(b) Agricultural credit system (refunds and new resources)	2.28	28.9
	(c) Others sources	1.90	24.1
	Total	7.88	100.0

A fact that must be particularly emphasized here is that the financial plan as it affects agriculture will depend to a great extent upon the planned repayment of loans, to an amount of 2.7 billion rubles. In view of the extremely weak organization of the system of agricultural credits and the unsatisfactory practice now prevailing in regard to the repayment of loans (not to mention the defects of the credit system in connection with deposits of peasants' savings), the utmost attention should be given to this aspect of agricultural financing.

The *plan of financing of electrical development* relies chiefly upon budgetary appropriations, as may be seen from the following estimates, including floating capital (in billions of rubles):

		Total for Five Years, 1928-29 to 1932-33	*Per Cent of Total*
1. Total funds required		3.10	100.0
2. Sources of financing:	(a) Government Budget	1.56	50.3
	(b) Own resources	0.54	17.4
	(c) Other sources	1.00	32.3
Total		3.10	100.0

The financial program of transportation is based upon the maintenance of railway rates, on the whole, at their present level, with a reduction of about 20 per cent in costs. In other words, there is provided a discrepancy between costs and rates, just as there is in industry between costs and prices. This method of financing in transportation is justified by the capital requirements in this field, on the one hand, and by the comparatively low level of rates, on the other. The general outlines of the financial plan for transportation are as follows, including floating capital (in billions of rubles):

	Total for Five Years, 1928-29 to 1932-33	Per Cent of Total
1. Total funds required	9.99	100.0
2. Sources of financing: (a) Resources of transportation	5.41	54.2
(b) Government budget	4.08	40.8
(c) Other sources	0.50	5.0
Total	9.99	100.0

It is thus seen that the budgetary grants for new development and for basic reconstruction in transportation are rather substantial, which is to be expected in view of the comparatively large scope of the development work provided in the five-year plan.

Housing construction included in the socialized sector will be financed essentially in the following manner (in billions of rubles), including floating capital:

	Total for Five Years, 1928-29 to 1932-33	Per Cent of Total
1. Total funds required	4.03	100.0
2. Sources of financing: (a) Resources of economic organizations	1.44	35.7
(b) Social insurance funds	0.76	18.9
(c) Other sources	1.83	45.4
Total	4.03	100.0

Finally, *social welfare and cultural services* (education, public health service and social insurance) are to be financed chiefly from two sources, the government budget and the social insurance funds. The essential figures relating to this group are as follows (in billions of rubles), including floating capital:

	Total for Five Years, 1928-29 to 1932-33	*Per Cent of Total*
1. Total funds required	21.55	100.0
2. Sources of financing: (a) Government budget	10.88	50.5
(b) Social insurance funds	8.45	39.2
(c) Other sources	2.22	10.3
Total	21.55	100.0

Above has been given only the barest outlines of the financial program drawn up for the five-year period. However, this general summary indicates that the five-year economic plan is to be carried out with the aid of the same financial methods that have been built up in the preceding five-year period. There is, nevertheless, this difference that, whereas up to this time the various elements of the financial system have been, to a great extent, functioning independently of one another, they will now be firmly bound together in a single financial plan. This will not obviate the necessity, even during the process of carrying out the tasks set by the plan, of inquiring into the matter of a general revision of the financial system, with a view to adapting it more perfectly to the conditions and requirements of the upbuilding of a socialist economic system.

In dealing with the financial estimates for the five-year period, the reservation must constantly be borne in mind that they are conditioned and dependent upon all other aspects of the plan. As the work of filling in further practical details of the plan progresses, and as the yearly economic plans are worked out, the financial program will be supplemented through additional studies and, in particular, the problem of carrying out the program of cultural work to the limit will be taken up.

It should be strongly emphasized that the principal difficulty in connection with the financial program lies not in the drawing up of a general balance for the five-year period as a whole, but in the financing of those construction and production objectives which must be attained in the early years of the period, and whose realization is, to a great extent, a condition of the success of the five-year plan, both in regard to its scope and to the tempo of economic development. The greatest financial acumen must, therefore, be exercised with a view primarily to meeting the problems of the first few years, which will be the most responsible and difficult ones to be faced.

One of the great objectives of the five-year plan is the accumulation of reserves in the process of economic development. In the preceding chapter there was indicated the solution of the problem of reserves of fuel, grain, stocks of commodities. The plan provides, in all these lines, not only for alleviation of the present shortages, but even for a considerable increase in reserves. The same policy has been followed in regard to the financial plan as a whole and to the program of currency issue, in particular, both of which have been drawn up with extreme caution. Here again, the first years of the period will, of course, be the most difficult ones.

CHAPTER IX

THE SOCIAL PROGRAM

EVERY economic plan in the Soviet Union, and especially a general plan of national economy for a period of five years, must supply the clearest answer to the question as to *what extent the realization of the plan will serve to strengthen the socialist elements in the economic system of the country.*

In the preceding chapters it has been very plainly indicated that the dominating idea of the entire five-year plan is the industrialization of the Soviet Union—that industrial development which is the only possible and solid foundation for the growth of the socialist elements. The character of the development program, the apportionment of capital investments and the resulting structure of the basic capital, the planned rates of increase of production, the scope of the development in the socialized sector of agriculture, the distribution of the national income,—all these elements are directly and consistently subordinated to the central idea of the plan, which points out the way to the intensive growth of the productive forces of the country through industrialization, through socialist reorganization of rural life, through systematic socialization of every field and process of economic life.

The most general indicators of the progress of socialization, as outlined in the five-year plan, may be summarized as follows:

SHARE OF THE SOCIALIZED (STATE AND COOPERATIVE) SECTOR
(in per cent of total)

	1927-28	*1932-33*
	Per Cent	
(1) Number of persons working for hire	79.9	83.9
(2) Basic capital	52.7	68.9
(3) Capital investments	57.7	83.7
(4) Gross production, industrial and agricultural	45.9	66.5
Including:		
(a) agricultural	1.8	14.7
(b) industrial	79.5	92.4
(5) Retail trade	75.0	91.1
(6) National income	52.7	66.3

Concomitant with the expansion of state-controlled industry, the large construction program and the great increase in production, primarily in the socialized sector, there will take place a rapid growth of cities. The urban population, which formed 18.4 per cent of the total in 1927-28, will exceed 20 per cent in 1932-33. The progress of socialist development will undoubtedly give rise to very important problems in regard to the change in the very character of cities. But irrespective of this, the increase in the relative numerical importance of the city population, which means, above all, an increase in the relative importance of the proletariat in relation to the total population, will in itself be both a significant indication of and a serious factor in the growing strength of the socialist elements of the country.

The share of the socialized sector in the total volume of production will increase very considerably. In 1924-25 that share was 29.8 per cent of the total agricultural and industrial production, in 1927-28 it rose to 46 per cent, and at the end of the five-year period it is expected to reach 66.5 per cent. Of particular significance is the increase of the share of the socialized sector in agriculture, which will, according to the plan, increase from 1.8 per cent in 1927-28 to nearly 15 per cent in 1932-33.

Of decisive importance from the standpoint of a radical reconstruction of the entire economic system of the country, is the *distribution of capital investments and the resulting changes in the structure of basic capital. The share of the total amount of capital investments which will go into the socialized fields will rise from 57.7 per cent in 1927-28 to nearly 84 per cent in 1932-33. Accordingly, the basic capital funds of the socialized sector will have increased from 52.7 per cent of the total basic capital to 69 per cent. Within the socialized sector itself there will be a considerable increase in the share of basic capital invested in industry.*

The development of the socialized sector in agriculture will put its impress on the entire social program for the five years. It is here that the chief distinction lies between the present five-year plan and all similar general plans drawn up in the past. The acreage in the socialized sector in agriculture (on state and cooperative farms) will be increased by the spring of 1933 to 26 million hectares, and will thus form over 18 per cent of the total area under cultivation in the country. By the end of the five-year period (crop of 1932) 19.8 per cent of the total grain output and 43 per cent of the marketable portion, will come from state and collective farms. About 20 million peasants will by then be enlisted in the socialized sector, which will mean a virtual cessation in the increase of the peasant population in the private sector. All this taken together will bring an entirely new principle into the very structure of agricultural production and of peasant life, in general. With machine technique and with the use of scientific methods as its base, the socialized sector in agriculture will be the driving force for a gradual socialist reorganization of agriculture as a whole. On the five-year period now under consideration falls the great task of establishing one of the most important milestones along this road.

A significant factor in the strengthening of the socialist element in national economy is cooperative organization, which has already become one of the principal agencies of socialization, not only in the sphere of distribution, but in production as well. The five-year plan provides for a further strengthening of cooperation and of its part in all those fields of economy where this form of organization is called for, in order to socialize small-scale production. The following are the most essential figures illustrating the progress of cooperation:

	1927-28	1932-33
A. Extension of cooperative production:		
(1) Share of cooperative farming in total grain production, per cent	1.0	15.5
(2) Share of small industrial cooperatives in total output of all small industry, per cent	19.4	53.8
B. Extension of cooperative trade:		
(1) Share of cooperative retail trade in total retail trade, per cent	60.2	78.9
C. Extension of cooperative membership:		
(1) Peasant households affiliated with agricultural cooperatives, number in thousands of households	9,500	23,580
Per cent	37.5	85.0
(2) Membership of consumers' cooperatives		
(a) Urban, number in millions	8.7	16.5
Per cent of adult population	45.3	70.0
(b) Rural, number in millions	13.9	31.8
Per cent of adult population	19.1	40.0
(3) Membership of producers' cooperatives, in small trades, number in millions	0.9	3.7
Per cent of the total number engaged in small trades	21.0	56.0

It is obvious that *all these ways and methods of fortifying the socialist elements in national economy,* whether in regard to production or to capital investments, to the movement of basic capital, to the development of the socialized sector in agriculture, to cooperation, etc., *will prove adequate as instruments of socialization only in the measure that the great increase of efficiency in the socialized sector is carried out as planned.* That is why such objectives as a 35 per cent reduction in industrial production costs, a 20 per cent reduction in transportation costs, a 50 per cent reduction in costs of industrial construction, the doubling of the crop yields in state farms as compared with individual farms, etc., are not only important as economic achievements, but also as powerful instruments in the solution of the social problems of the five-year period.

The movement and the structure of the national income are among the most general and the most important indicators of the nature of the economic plan, as a whole, and of its social aspects, in particular. The national income will increase during the five-year period from 24.7 billion rubles in 1927-28 to 43.3 billion in 1932-33, if computed at prices of that year, or to 49.7 billion at constant prices, an increase of 75 per cent or 103 per cent, respectively. This means an *increase in the total national income at an annual rate of over 10 per cent, and a per capita increase of over 7 per cent, a rate three times as high as that of the increase in national income in pre-revolutionary Russia, and greatly exceeding that observed in all other advanced countries.* The greatest increase of per capita income thus far recorded anywhere was in the United States in the period from 1880 to 1890, when it amounted to 58 per cent, or at the rate of about 4.5 per cent a year. In the quarter of a century preceding the war the per capita income in the advanced capitalist countries showed practically no increase (1.2 per cent a year in the United States, about 0.2 per cent in Germany, no increase in England), while in the Soviet Union, in the period

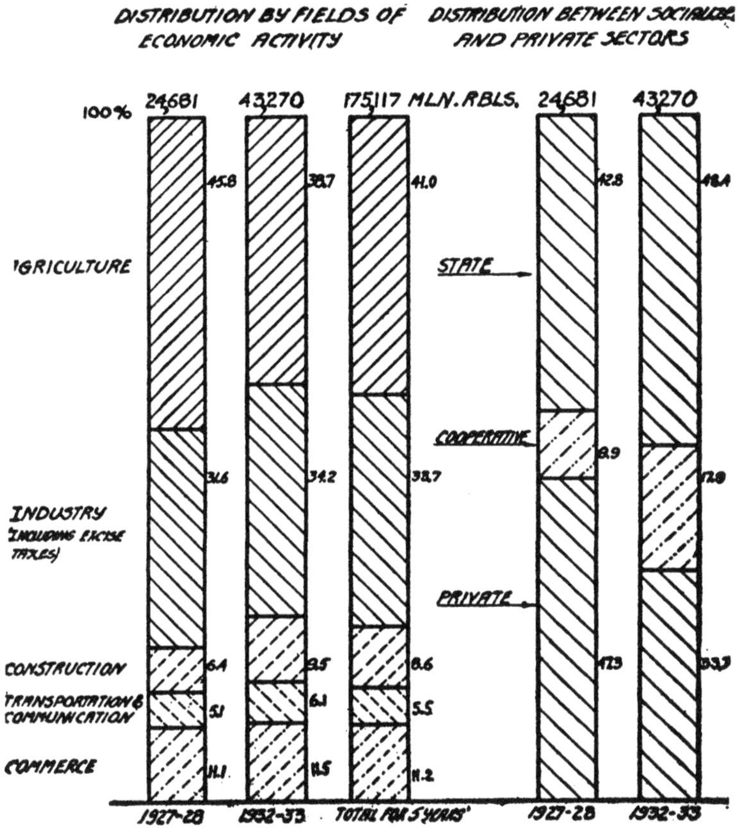

DISTRIBUTION OF THE NATIONAL INCOME IN THE U.S.S.R.
(Net Production at Prices of Respective Years, Per Cent of Total)

from 1924-25 to 1927-28, the per capita income increased 31 per cent, or at an annual rate of about 10 per cent. At the same rate of growth, the per capita income in 1928-29 will attain 116 per cent of pre-war, and by the end of the five-year period it should reach at least 170 per cent of the 1913 income. It is superfluous to dwell at length on the importance of this increase in income in the five-year period under consideration, both from the practical and theoretical standpoints. The socialist economic system opens up possibilities for the development of productive forces which are now no longer available in countries where a different system prevails.

The changes in the *distribution of national income* by the main divisions of production may be seen from the following table (percentages of total):

	At Prices of Respective Years		*At Prices of 1926-27*	
	1927-28	*1932-33*	*1927-28*	*1932-33*
		Per Cent		
Agriculture	45.8	38.7	44.1	33.6
Industry, total (including excises)	31.6	34.2	32.7	38.2
Of which:				
Large scale industry (including excises)	26.6	30.4	27.7	34.2
Construction	6.4	9.5	6.8	11.8
Other fields	16.2	17.6	16.4	16.4
	100.0	100.0	100.0	100.0

The progress of industrialization is clearly reflected in this movement of national income. The share of construction will increase simultaneously with that of industry. It should be noted that the share of agriculture in the national income is somewhat lower when figured at constant prices than when taken at the current prices in the respective years, whereas the situation in regard to industry is just the reverse. This circumstance is a reflection of the price policy, which is designed to maintain agricultural prices at a nearly stable level, while reducing the prices of industrial products. It results also in the agricultural output, taken by itself, holding a somewhat larger place in the sphere of distribution than in production.

Just as the distribution of the national income by divisions of production reflects the industrial process, *its distribution between the private and the socialized sectors reflects the rapid progress of socialization.* In 1924-25 the share of the socialized sector in the formation of the national income was only about 31 per cent, in 1927-28 it rose to nearly 53 per cent, and by the end of the five-year period it is expected to exceed 66 per cent. In other words, by that time *two-thirds of the net production of the country will come from the socialized sector.*

The national income (net production) per capita of population will increase from 163 rubles in 1927-28 to 256 rubles in 1932-33, *an increase of 57 per cent in five years.* The total income accruing to individuals is estimated to show an increase of 76 per cent in the five years.

Finally, of great interest and significance are the changes anticipated by the plan in the per capita money and real incomes of the urban and the rural population, respectively. These changes may be illustrated by the following figures:

PER CAPITA INCREASE IN FIVE YEARS

	Money Incomes	*Real Incomes*
	Per Cent	
Non-agricultural population	47	71
Of whom:		
Persons working for hire ...	52	77
Agricultural population	37	67
Of whom:		
Peasants in collective farming	50	83
Peasants in individual enterprises	33	62
Agricultural proletariat	47	79

The increase in the income of the peasant population has been probably somewhat underestimated here, due to the method used in computing peasant incomes from occupations other than agriculture. It may be safe to assume, therefore, that the real improvement in the standards of living of the urban and of the rural population will proceed at about the same rate, with the incomes of the proletariat, both in the city and in the country, increasing much more rapidly than those of the total population. In other words, the carrying out of the plan will bring to an end the further growth of the discrepancy between the urban and the rural standards of living, and by this very fact will make a good start toward its gradual elimination, which is one of the most important objects of socialism. In addition, this same development is of prime importance in solving the immediate problem of furthering a rapid increase in agricultural production within the first years of the period covered by the plan.

Such are, in general outline, the most important elements in the social program for the five years. Each of these elements, as well as the social program as a whole, will mark a steady advance of the socialist elements in the economic system of the Soviet Union. *If the general development program may justifiably be called a plan of great works, the social program is a plan of a fully developed socialist offensive on the entire front of economic development of the country. It is here that the strength of the five-year plan lies.*

CHAPTER X

FOREIGN TRADE[1]

1. EXPORT

In the general five-year plan of foreign trade the export plan is of primary importance, inasmuch as it is exports that supply the resources needed to meet the country's requirements of imported goods.

Under the provisions of the plan, exports will increase almost 165 per cent in the five years and will attain a total of 2,047 million rubles in 1932-33, as against 774 million rubles in 1927-28. As compared with the pre-war export trade in the territory now constituting the Soviet Union, exports in 1932-33 will show an increase of 22 per cent (1,600 million rubles at pre-war prices, as against 1,307 millions on the average for the years 1909-1913). For the five-year period as a whole the aggregate value of exports will amount to 7 billion rubles, at current prices of the respective years.

The planning of an expansion of exports at this rapid tempo is made possible by the profound changes in the production system which have been provided by the

[1] This chapter is a summary of articles on the five-year plan of foreign trade in the Voprosy Torgovly (Problems of Trade) for May, 1929.

plan, and which also determine the nature and the distribution of the export trade. The structure of exports in the five-year period will reflect the changes to be effected in the national economy as a whole. The most essential economic process, which is the industrialization of the Soviet Union, will find reflection likewise in the export plan, as may be seen from the following comparative figures showing the relative importance of agricultural and industrial exports, in percentages of total exports:

	1909-13	*1932-33*
	Per Cent	
Agricultural exports	80.8	50.5
Industrial exports	19.2	49.5

The distribution of the basic elements in the Soviet export trade will thus differ essentially from that of pre-war exports, just as the entire economic structure of the Soviet Union will differ radically from that of the old Russian Empire.

It may be asked whether such an increase in the relative importance of industrial exports does not mean an abandonment of the policy of developing agricultural exports or at least a retardation of this development. There is no ground for such apprehensions. Just as the general industrialization of the Soviet Union does not in any degree imply a suspension of agricultural development and, on the contrary, provides for its further progress and reconstruction on new technical and social bases, with industry playing a leading rôle, so the industrialization of exports will be combined with a simultaneous growth of agricultural exports in new forms, those of "refined" and processed agricultural products. The quantitative statement of this process is given by the following figures: In the five-year period from 1928-29 to 1932-33 industrial exports will increase 159 per cent (from 392 million rubles in 1927-28 to 1,014 millions in 1932-33), while agricultural exports will in the same period increase 170 per cent (from 382 to 1,033 million rubles). Thus, agricultural exports, besides showing a great increase, as compared with the present time, in absolute amounts will also assume greater importance in the total exports.

This last-mentioned point can be explained by the situation as regards the development of *grain exports.* Indeed, if grain is not included, the changes in the relative importance of agricultural and industrial exports will appear quite different, as may be seen from the following table (per cent of total exports):

	Including Grain		*Not Including Grain*	
	1927-28	*1932-33*	*1927-28*	*1932-33*
Agricultural exports	49.4	50.5	45.4	36.9
Industrial exports	50.6	49.5	54.6	63.1

In the last two years the elimination of grain from the Soviet exports resulted in a much larger decrease of the relative importance of the total agricultural exports than would have been caused by the growth of industrial exports alone. This situation will have been remedied by the end of the five-year period and, as a result, the relative importance of all agricultural exports, including grain, will be even somewhat increased, while the share of industrial products in the total exports other than grain will continue to grow.

Contrary to the condition prevailing in the last few years, by 1932-33 the Soviet Union will be a substantial grain exporter. This is in full conformity with the objectives which the five-year plan sets for agriculture and, especially, for grain farming, and with the social and economic processes outlined in the plan. The increased yield of grain combined with an extended acreage, will guarantee the possibility of increasing grain exports, while at the same time the growing demand of the domestic market will be met and the necessary stocks accumulated. The enlarged supply of fertilizers, live stock and tractors will be one of the most important factors in the increase of grain production.

Together with these factors, the development of state and collective farms will be of particular importance in its effects upon the export trade. The extension of the socialized sector will bring about an increase in the relative amount of the marketable portion of agricultural output, and this will not only result in making available for export additional grain supplies from the socialized sector, but will also furnish a firmer and more reliable basis for the realization of the export program, and will permit of a more effective control of the grade and condition of the exported grain. To attain this end it is necessary, of course, in the organization of state farms, to take into due consideration geographical conditions, in order to assure their proper distribution by regions producing grain for the domestic market and those producing for export.

Notwithstanding the fact, however, that the grain export will show both an absolute and a relative growth in the five years, and that its share in the total exports will accordingly become larger than at present, it will still be considerably lower than in pre-war years, amounting to 24.7 per cent of all exports in 1932-33 as against 53.2 per cent on the average in the years 1909 to 1913. Grain exports will to a great extent give way to products of intensive farming, on the one hand, and to industrial products, on the other.

The distribution of Soviet exports by general groups of commodities at the end of the five-year period is shown in the table on the page opposite.

Separate mention should be made of the development of so-called "secondary exports," which will mean a considerable extension of the export basis of the Soviet Union in the five years. A number of industries and agricultural activities which thus far have been only slightly related to the export trade will gradually acquire during the five-year period growing importance as sources of Soviet exports.

In order to assure a regular and steady development of the export trade and to provide the necessary technical equipment for export marketing, large amounts of capital will be invested in the construction of elevators, warehouses, plants for the primary treatment of agricultural products, refrigerators, sorting plants, etc. Considerable sums are to be allotted for the development of industries in Siberia and in the Far East working for export.

DISTRIBUTION OF EXPORTS

	1927-28	*1932-33*		*Ratio of 1932-33 to 1927-28*
	Million Rubles	*Million Rubles*	*Per Cent of Total*	*Per Cent*
Agricultural Exports				
Principal farm crops ..	95.3	543.5	26.6	570.3
Animal and poultry products	135.2	319.5	15.6	236.3
Hunting and fishery products	132.2	130.0	6.3	98.3
Other agricultural products	19.6	40.0	2.0	204.1
Total agricultural exports	382.3	1,033.0	50.5	270.2
Industrial Exports				
Forestry and mining products	230.5	678.4	33.1	294.3
Products of food and allied industries	48.7	99.6	4.9	204.5
Other industrial products	112.4	236.5	11.5	210.4
Total industrial exports	391.6	1,014.5	49.5	259.1
Grand total	773.9	2,047.5	100.0	264.6

The problem of capital investments in foreign trade is closely connected with that of the regional distribution of the sources of export. Capital investments will have to be coordinated with a proper geographical distribution of production for export, which in turn must be connected with an improvement in the quality of export goods. It will be well to examine these elements in relation to a few fundamental commodities.

As far as *grain* products are concerned, the principal exporting regions will have to be the Ukraine, the Crimea and the Northern Caucasus, in view of their proximity to the Black Sea ports. Grain supplies for the domestic market will have to come primarily from the eastern regions of the Soviet Union.

The regions assigned as sources of *lumber* export must be those best suited by their geographical location, as the forest area converging upon the White Sea ports, Karelia and the Leningrad district, the Far East, Transcaucasia, etc.

In regard to *petroleum* products one of the main objects in the immediate future should be more intensive prospecting in new districts in order to have new fields ready for exploitation by the end of the five-year period. At the same time, the petroleum industry has under consideration the problem of the distribution of the functions between the principal producing regions, namely, of assigning the domestic supply to the Emba district, while using the output of the Grozny and the Azerbaijan regions chiefly for export. The solution of this problem, to which so far only an approach has been made, may be of great value to the export trade.

In regard to *manganese,* it appears advisable to have the Chiaturi output as the main source of exports, inasmuch as that field has the advantages both of high quality ore and of a favorable location in regard to a port. The Nikopol district will have to work chiefly for the domestic market, only the surplus being exported across the land frontiers.

Likewise for a number of other commodities, including the so-called "secondary" exports, a proper regional distribution in accordance with export requirements is one of the requisites of successful work in the five-year period.

Another problem of the same order is that of the specialization of certain industrial establishments in the production of export articles. Such specialization, which is, of course, closely connected with regional distribution, will permit a great improvement in the quality of the goods and the attainment of the highest degree of standardization and uniformity of brands, which is of the greatest importance for the marketing of Soviet products abroad. This is a very great and intricate task, in view of the considerable volume to be attained by the export trade and the great changes to be effected in its nature, and also in view of the general situation in the world markets of the most important commodities as it may now be forecast, with all due reservations, for the five-year period.

An analysis of the export trade program of the five-year plan leads to the problem of further improvements in the export organization. To attain this a number of measures have been outlined, of which some of the more important will be mentioned. In the first place, the activities of the various procuring organizations[1] must be placed on a more effective basis, and the various regions and functions distributed among them in a rational manner. At the same time the stability of the structure of these organizations and agencies will have to be firmly established. It will further be necessary to proceed to the organization of a single selling agency for any commodities for which none now exists and for which it can be organized. A proper distribution of the spheres of activity and the specific tasks between the Soviet trade delegations abroad will have to be effected and they will have to be put into closer touch with the planning work of the People's Commissariat for Trade, in order to attain a complete coordination of plans. Trade connections with foreign companies and, in particular, with cooperative organizations, will also have to be strengthened

To summarize, it may be stated that the five-year economic plan adopted by the government contains sufficient guarantees as to the feasibility of the export program, and that it creates the conditions required for the accumulation of considerable stocks of commodities. In this manner there is provided the necessary basis for the drawing up of an import plan that shall meet the requirements of the national economy.

[1] Organizations either producing or purchasing products from domestic producers.

2. IMPORT

The problem of meeting the import requirements of the country has been one of the most important economic problems faced by the Soviet Union in the last few years. The industrialization of the country, which implies the most intensive effort in every field of economic activity, gives rise to the important task of satisfying the rapidly increasing requirements of industry.

The structure of the Soviet import trade at the present time is different in character, not only from the pre-war import trade, but also from that of the first years of reconstruction under the Soviet régime. The outstanding features are complete elimination of imports of luxuries, drastic economy in regard to imports of consumption goods, and a corresponding increase in the imports of goods for productive purposes. Out of the total imports in 1927-28, amounting to 945 million rubles, producers' goods made up 796 million rubles, or 84.3 per cent of the total. Imports of products for industry amounted to 718 million rubles, or 76.0 per cent of all imports.

In the five-year period from 1923 to 1928 imports into the Soviet Union aggregated 3,571 million rubles, of which 2,846 millions, or 79.7 per cent of the total, were imports of producers' goods, as may be seen from the table on the following page.

In spite of the fact that in the five-year period just elapsed imports of consumers' goods included flour in the poor crop year of 1924-25, producers' goods formed 79.7 per cent of all imports for the period, as against 63.5 per cent for the period 1909 to 1913. Imports of industrial equipment, in particular, have attained a large volume, and their share in the total imports far surpasses that of the pre-war period.

IMPORTS IN THE FIVE YEARS
1923-24 to 1927-28

	Millions of Rubles	*Percentage of Total*
1. Equipment	641.6	18.0
2. Raw materials	1,451.4	40.6
3. Semi-manufactures	546.8	15.3
4. Imports for needs of agriculture	189.3	5.3
5. Fuel	17.1	0.5
Total producers' goods	2,846.2	79.7
Total consumers' goods	685.1	19.2
Other imports	40.0	1.1
Total imports	3,571.3	100.0

Although the total volume of imports is confined within certain definite limits, it has been possible to secure the supply of imported goods required for the fundamental branches of national economy, and imports have played an important part in a number of industries, materially contributing to their growth. The share of imports in the total consumption of some of the most important commodities is about as follows: cotton, over 40 per cent; fine wool, over 90 per cent; copper, about 50 per cent; zinc, about 90 per cent; aluminum and nickel, 100 per cent. The greater part of the tractors required is now imported. Of all the equipment required in 1927-28 for capital construction in industry 27 per cent was imported. These figures show the importance of imports at the present time, both for industry as a whole and for some of the leading individual industries.

The great expansion of exports provided under the five-year plan permits the import program for 1932-33 to be set at 1,705 million rubles, representing an increase of 80 per cent over 1927-28. This rate of growth is considerably greater than that recorded prior to the war (50.6 per cent for the five-year period 1909 to 1913).

Producers' goods will continue to make up by far the greater part of all imports, and in this respect the situation will remain substantially unchanged. It will only be toward the end of the five-year period, as the import situation becomes less strained, that it will be possible to increase imports of consumers' goods, not only in absolute amounts, but in relation to total imports as well.

Within the group of producers' goods, there will be, in the course of the five-year period, a steady increase in imports of industrial and agricultural machinery, with a corresponding decrease in the relative importance of imported raw materials and semi-manufactures, which will be supplied to a growing extent from domestic sources.

THE FIVE-YEAR IMPORT PLAN

	1927-28		1932-33		Ratio of 1932-33 to 1927-28	Total for Five Years 1928-29 to 1932-33	
	Millions of Rubles	*Per Cent of Total*	*Millions of Rubles*	*Per Cent of Total*	*Per Cent*	*Millions of Rubles*	*Per Cent of Total*
1. Equipment for industry and transportation	256	27.1	525	30.8	205.1	1,784	28.8
2. Raw materials	384	40.7	523	30.8	136.2	2,047	33.1
3. Semi-manufactures	117	12.4	60	3.5	51.3	370	6.0
4. Agricultural requirements	39	4.1	165	9.6	423.1	622	10.1
Total Producers' Goods	796	84.3	1,273	74.7	159.9	4,823	78.0
1. Articles of general consumption	120	12.7	250	14.6	208.3	814	13.2
2. Medical and sanitary articles	10.5	1.1	12	0.7	114.3	45	0.7
3. Cultural requirements	12.5	1.3	20	1.2	160.0	66	1.1
Total Consumers' Goods	143	15.1	282	16.5	197.2	925	15.0
Other imports	6	0.6	150	8.8	....	432	7.0
Total imports	945	100.0	1,705	100.0	180.0	6,180	100.0

This tendency toward the lessening of dependence upon imports can best be observed in the movement of imports of the group of semi-manufactured goods. In the past few years it has been already possible to reduce this group of imports, notwithstanding the expansion of industry, and a further reduction is provided under the five-year plan. A number of semi-manufactures, as yarn, paper, etc., will no longer be on the import list by the end of the five-year period, as a result of the growth of domestic production. As the chemical and other industries are built up, the need for imported dyes, chemicals, tanning materials, and a number of other semi-manufactures will sharply decrease in the course of the five-year plan.

The development and the reconstruction of agriculture in general, and of the production of industrial crops, in particular, at the rates provided under the plan, naturally warrant the assumption that the dependence upon imported raw materials will also diminish, although not to the same extent as in regard to semi-manufactures.

Substantial achievements in the way of developing domestic resources of raw materials are expected in regard to non-ferrous metals, as will be seen from the figures on the following page.

The decrease in the relative importance of imports in the total consumption of non-ferrous metals will result from the rapid development of the metal industry. The output of copper smelters in 1932-33 will be more

SHARE OF DOMESTIC AND IMPORTED PRODUCTS
IN THE CONSUMPTION OF NON-FERROUS METALS IN THE SOVIET UNION
(Percentages of Total Consumption)

	Copper		*Zinc*		*Lead*		*Aluminum*		*Nickel*	
	1927-28	*1932-33*	*1927-28*	*1932-33*	*1927-28*	*1932-33*	*1927-28*	*1932-33*	*1927-28*	*1932-33*
1. Domestic supplies	50.1	59.0	9.8	79.5	5.9	38.9	....	46.7	....	55.6
2. Imports	49.9	41.0	90.2	20.5	94.1	61.1	100.0	53.3	100.0	44.4
3. Total consumption	100.0	100.0	100.0	100.0	100.0	100.0	100.0	100.0	100.0	100.0

than three times that of 1927-28, the production of lead will increase tenfold, that of zinc more than twenty times, etc.

As far as raw materials of agricultural origin are concerned, considerable attention is given by the five-year plan to the development of cotton cultivation. Cotton is at the present time the most important article among the imports of raw materials, and the present output of the cotton goods industry is insufficient to meet the demand of the population. The intensive promotion of cotton growing at a rapid rate is designed to guarantee the development of the Soviet cotton goods industry on the basis of domestic raw materials. The provisions of the five-year plan in this regard are based upon the estimates of the agricultural division of the State Planning Commission, according to which the production of cotton in 1932-33 will be two and one-half times that of 1927-28. As a result of this growth of domestic cotton production, imported cotton will form by the end of the five-year period only about 10 per cent of the total industrial consumption, as against 42.5 per cent in 1927-28. This development of the cotton industry is connected with the program of large capital investments in irrigation.

The situation in regard to hides is different. The share of imports in the total supply will not only not decrease in the five years, but will even increase somewhat. The growth of the domestic supplies of hides as provided under the plan will be insufficient to meet fully the requirements of the expanding leather industry, and the need for imported hides will, therefore, still remain considerable by the end of the five-year period.

In view of the great projected expansion of the woolen industry in the five years ahead, with the output of woolen cloths in 1932-33 amounting to about 280 per cent of that of 1927-28, no great diminution in the relative importance of imported wool may be expected. The development of fine fleece sheep raising as planned for the five-year period will be insufficient to cover the shortage of fine wool; the real effects of this development will be felt only after the expiration of the five years, while in the period from 1928-29 to 1932-33 imports of wool will remain considerable.

The necessity of greater economy in the imports of raw materials in the five-year period is particularly great in view of the formidable problems faced by the import trade in supplying equipment on a sufficient scale to keep pace with the development work in industry and in transportation. The aggregate imports of industrial equipment for the five years will amount to about 1,800 million rubles.

Parallel with the great expansion of imports for industrial requirements, the five-year plan provides for a very considerable growth of imports for the needs of agriculture. The expansion and reconstruction of agriculture, involving increase in crop yields, organization of state and collective farms on a great scale, development of the production of agricultural raw materials, will call for tremendous efforts in order to guarantee an adequate supply of agricultural machinery, tractors, etc. Whereas, a considerable increase is planned in the domestic production of tractors and attachments, it will be insufficient to meet the requirements in the five-year period.

The plan in regard to tractor production provides for an output of 50,000 tractors in 1932-33, and for 85,200 for the five-year period. At least as many more will have to be imported, even if only the minimum program of tractor supply is to be carried out, according to which the number of tractors in use in the country by the end of 1932-33 will reach 160,000 as against 38,000 tractors in use at the present time. Imports of tractors and attachments in the five years will run into hundreds of millions of rubles.

Imports of fertilizers will likewise have to continue in the five years under consideration, in spite of the great increase in domestic production.

The total value of imports for the needs of agriculture will aggregate over 600 million rubles during the period. This figure is sufficient to indicate the important rôle to be played by imports as a factor of agricultural reconstruction and progress. The volume of imports planned represents the minimum required in order to carry out the program of agricultural development for the five years. The efficiency with which these imports will be utilized, will depend entirely upon the timely preparation of a technical basis for the operation of imported tractors, upon a thorough study of the kinds of fertilizers required in the several regions, upon their proper distribution and so on. The accelerated development of the domestic fertilizer industry may bring about a gradual reduction in imports of fertilizers by the end of the five-year period, only on the condition, however, that every effort be exerted to carry out the production plans fully within the assigned time limits.

The growth of imports of consumers' goods will affect mainly imports from Oriental countries, and it will be furthered by the great increase in Soviet exports to those countries. Imports of consumers' goods from the East may be expected to attain more than one and one-half times their present volume by the end of the five-year period. A considerable increase is expected in the imports of such articles as tea, the consumption of which is now somewhat below that of prewar times, coffee, cocoa, oranges, lemons, etc., due to the improvement in the general standard of living.

While the country's requirements of imported goods will be much more nearly satisfied at the conclusion of the five-year period than at present, the plan also anticipates a favorable trade balance, which is essential to assure an uninterrupted development of foreign trade and to provide improved conditions for foreign trade activities abroad. The favorable trade balance for the five years from 1928-29 to 1932-33 will aggregate about 800 million rubles.

Such are the main outlines of the development of imports planned for the five years. Its outstanding features are an extension of relations with the world markets, combined with a lesser dependence upon them of the basic parts of Soviet economy, a general improvement in the supplying of imported commodities to consumers, and an increase of stocks and of foreign exchange reserves.

These results will be attained only at the end of the five-year period. In the few years immediately ahead the present strain in the import trade and the difficulties resulting from the generally narrow limits of import possibilities will be gradually done away with as exports increase. In order to meet the import requirements of the fundamental branches of national economy, every effort will have to be exerted in the next few years to further the movement of exports, to expand those branches of domestic production which may, within a short time, supply substitutes for imports, and to economize in the consumption of imported goods.

The effective utilization of the enormous quantity of machinery which is to be imported under the plan will depend, to a great extent, upon a better planning of imports. Industry must undertake the task of drawing up, within the specified time, the plans of delivery and of utilization of imported machinery, in accordance with the construction program and with the technical specifications of the machinery to be imported

The work on the further elaboration of the five-year plan will have to deal with the conditions required for the most efficient and rational utilization of the six billion odd rubles which, under the plan, will be expended abroad during the period in payment for imports.

APPENDIX I

THE SYSTEM OF ECONOMIC PLANNING IN THE SOVIET UNION[1]

The state planning system in the Soviet Union embraces all fields of national economy, although not all fields have as yet been socialized to the same extent. By socialized field is understood one under the control and direction either of a state economic body, or of a cooperative organization. Thus, for instance, railway and water transportation, the large manufacturing industries, the electrification system and foreign trade, are almost entirely controlled and administered by state agencies. Other branches of economy, such as agriculture and domestic trade, are in part socialized under state and cooperative control, while the remaining part still remains under private ownership. The general tendency, however, running all through the economic policy of the Soviet Union, is toward a steady extension of socialization.

In planning for the socialized part of the national economy of the Soviet Union the guiding principle is the rational will applied with a view to securing the highest degree of economic and cultural development and the proper utilization of the returns from this part

[1] This section has been prepared by the editors of the English translation of the Five-Year Plan.

of the national economy, based upon a preliminary estimate both of the requirements and of the available resources.

As regards planning in the other part of national economy, still under private control, it is here reduced to estimating possible prospects on the basis of past experience of economic development and of possible future tendencies, including also the probable effects of the socialized sector upon private economy. In other words, the work of planning in the private sector deals with all those elements found in capitalist economy, together with the modifying influence of the socialized sector.

What are the results achieved by planning? An answer to this question may be supplied by any large corporation in a highly industrial country which controls, in a considerable measure, the production and distribution of a certain product, whether it be steel, or copper, or oil, etc. Such a corporation is in a position to estimate to a certain extent the needs of the market, to correlate its production with these needs and to secure the greatest advantages of large scale production. Centralization and general planning of production result in lower costs of management and permit the introduction of large plant equipment, which results in cheaper, faster and simplified processes of production. In distribution, concentration and centralization bring about a faster, more intensive, and less expensive circulation of goods, and reduce sales and advertising outlays.

However, in a capitalist economy, while an individual company may plan its own operations in an exemplary manner, all enterprises are at the mercy of the elemental forces of the market, as a result of the inherent antagonism between the great number of individual plans. This element of contradiction between plans is absent in the socialized sector of Soviet economy. The Soviet economic system is not designed to enrich certain groups of persons, but is a state economic system, whose aim is to steadily develop and enrich the country as a whole, while maintaining a proper proportion in the development of the various branches of economy. This opens up great possibilities to individual Soviet organizations, and affords them considerable advantages, as compared with individual private capitalist enterprises, in the way of enabling them to operate in accordance with a rational plan, drawn up in coordination with all other Soviet economic plans, instead of operating on a basis of competition, which, in view of the antagonism between individual enterprises, would mean the undermining of the very principle of general planning.

The socialization of Soviet economy, its centralization, the planning of both production and trade under a single system, and the centralized financing of economic activities—these are the instruments employed in the Soviet Union for making production and distribution economical in the highest possible degree. This is attained through the creation of state trusts, combinations and syndicates, the construction of large enterprises, through centralized management guided by a general plan, and the systematic policy of gradually distributing the various industries by economic regions, in accordance with the raw materials and fuel available in each region.

Since the Soviet Union has a unified, coordinated and planned economy, and the government is in a position to divert resources from one branch of economy to another, the possibility of a breakdown in any particular sector is precluded. This accounts for the fact that in the course of their commercial relations with foreign countries, not a single instance of failure of Soviet organizations to meet their obligations has been noted.

Organized economic administration in the Soviet Union is effected by means of planning concentrated in a single government agency, the State Planning Commission (Gosplan). The plans now in force in the economic system of the Soviet Union embrace periods of varying length. General plans covering the national economy as a whole are drawn for periods of five years and one year.

The five-year plan outlines the course of the entire national economy, and of the various fields of economic activity—production, distribution, finances, etc. It takes into consideration all aspects of economic and cultural development in the period covered and determines the volume and the character of production, distribution and financing, with a view to attaining the most rapid rate of development in the most economical manner. It also endeavors to secure the most harmonious balance between the various phases of economic activity by eliminating all factors which might tend to disturb this balance.

The annual plans relating to the entire national economy of the country are prepared much in the same manner and with the same objects in view, but are of a more concrete and specific nature. In addition, separate plans of still more detailed character are drawn up annually and quarterly for the several fields of economic activity, and monthly for individual enterprises.

The preparation of plans is carried out on the basis of the general instructions issued by the State Planning Commission of the Soviet Union. The specific data relating to the several economic fields and to individual enterprises are worked out on the spot, by the economic agencies of the several provinces, regions, autonomous and constituent republics, by the various government departments having economic functions, and, finally, by the individual enterprises themselves. All these specific data are then combined by the State Planning Commission and coordinated into a single general plan of economic administration. After ratification by the higher authorities the annual or the five-year plan of national economy becomes legally effective as the guiding rule of all economic activities of the country.

The enforcement of the plan is effected under the direction and supervision of the government departments in the various fields of economic activity of the Soviet Union and of the several constituent republics (Supreme Council of National Economy, People's Commissariat for Trade, People's Commissariats for Agriculture, etc.), with the active participation of state trusts and syndicates, local economic and administrative agencies, and also of civic organizations embracing the masses of the people. It is due to the keen interest, the enthusiasm, and the tremendous efforts displayed by the working masses of the U.S.S.R. in the furthering of economic reconstruction since the revolution, that the country, once almost wrecked and ruined, has become a sound economic organism capable of further intensive growth. This indicates that in the future, also, the work of national construction can be successfully accomplished only through the support of the working masses and their participation in the work through such organizations as labor unions, factory conferences, clubs, etc., through the discussion of the formidable problems confronting the country, and through direct representation of the workers in the administrative and supervisory bodies.

The question may be asked, to what extent are Soviet plans confirmed by actual developments? It cannot be expected, of course, that any economic plan will be 100 per cent completely carried out, with absolute precision and without deviations in any direction, especially when the plan is drawn for a considerable period ahead and embraces the entire economic life of such a big country as the Soviet Union, with all the complex interplay of the most varied economic factors. The object of the plans is not to predict, by means of detailed estimates, and with absolute precision, the course of economic developments in all particulars, but to determine the basic guiding lines and the general scope of the economic efforts to be exerted in the period under consideration.

The five-year plan of national economy of the Soviet Union, which was prepared by the State Planning Commission for the period from 1926-27 to 1930-31 made the following estimates of the total gross volume of production in industry and agriculture (at pre-war prices) [1]:

1926-27..................	18.8	billion	rubles
1927-28..................	20.2	"	"
1928-29..................	21.6	"	"
1929-30..................	22.9	"	"
1930-31..................	24.3	"	"

Due to the enormous efforts exerted for the furthering of economic development, these estimates were

[1] "Perspectives for the Development of National Economy of the U.S.S.R. for 1926-27 to 1930-31," published by the State Planning Commission of the U.S.S.R., 1927. Tables 2 and 3.

greatly surpassed in the first two years. In 1926-27 the gross output of industry and agriculture attained (at pre-war prices) a total of 21.1 billion rubles, or 2.3 billions in excess of the estimate, and in 1927-28 it reached 22.3 billion rubles, or 2.1 billions above the estimate. For the succeeding years the potentialities of economic development appear to exceed the estimates of the former plan to an even greater extent. The present five-year plan, for the period from 1928-29 to 1932-33, takes into account, with all possible completeness and precision, these increased possibilities of economic progress of the Soviet Union along the road of industrialization and socialist development.

As regards the sources of financing new construction work, production, and trade in the period under consideration, the present plan is based almost entirely upon the utilization of resources accumulated within the country. The part assigned (in the financing of development and production projects) to foreign capital invested in concessions is altogether insignificant, hardly amounting to one per cent of all new basic capital investments for the five years. In regard to foreign trade the financing of imports will likewise be covered almost entirely from the proceeds of Soviet exports, with foreign credits playing only a very small part. Under the plan, exports will greatly exceed imports in the five-year period as a whole (exports of 7 billion rubles as against imports of 6 billion rubles).

The national economy of the Soviet Union has been

reconstructed and developed at a rapid tempo in the last few years without the aid of foreign capital, and this process of intensive development can proceed in the same manner in the future at the rapid pace provided by the five-year plan. Should there be, however, a considerable flow of foreign capital into the Soviet Union, in the shape of loans or of investments in Soviet enterprises, the result would be a rate of economic development even more rapid than that provided under the plan, with a corresponding increase during the five-year period in the volume of foreign trade, and of imports, in particular, above the estimates given above.

The enormous natural resources of the Soviet Union, the rational economic policy in force, and the consistent effort toward industrialization, which involves many large-scale construction projects—all these combine to make the Soviet Union at the present time probably the greatest potential market in the world for industrial equipment and the most extensive field for the application of foreign capital. In 1927-28 imports of industrial and transportation equipment into the Soviet Union amounted to 256 million rubles, and it is estimated that they will aggregate over 1,800 million rubles in the five years covered by the plan. In addition, agricultural machinery and implement imports will amount to about 600 million rubles. These imports may reach a much higher figure if the expansion of Soviet imports is aided by large long-term foreign loans.

As the plan of reconstruction and of new development in industry and agriculture is carried out, the United States may well prove to be the most important of all countries as a source of Soviet imports, for the following reason. As industrial production in the Soviet Union is concentrated in large enterprises and is based on the principle of standardized mass production, American machines and machine tools are the most suitable, since their construction and design is likewise adapted, in type and in volume, for large plants and standardized production. Besides, American machines are technically superior to the European product in many ways. As the largest producer of improved agricultural machinery of various kinds, the United States will also play an important part in the mechanization of Soviet agriculture.

It is obvious that the economic development of the Soviet Union, insofar as it involves the technical reconstruction of industry and of agriculture, will insistently dictate imports of considerably increased quantities of instruments of production. Imports of raw materials (cotton, non-ferrous metals, rosin, etc.) will also be continued.

The influence of American technique will also penetrate into Soviet national economy in other ways besides the importation of American machinery, namely, by making American technical training and experience available for Soviet industries by means of technical assistance contracts with large American concerns, through engaging American experts for work in the U.S.S.R. and delegating special Soviet commissions and individual specialists to the United States to study American production methods on the spot, through demonstrations of American machinery sent to the U.S.S.R. and, finally, through the establishment of American enterprises in the Soviet Union on a concession basis.

TABLE I

BASIC INDICATORS OF THE ECONOMIC DEVELOPMENT OF THE SOVIET UNION UNDER THE FIVE-YEAR PLAN

	1927–28	1932–33	*Total for 5 Years*	*Ratio of* 1932–33 *to* 1927–28 *Per cent*
I. *Population* (millions):				
(1) Total (as on April 1)	151.3	169.2	......	111.8
Including:				
Urban	27.9	34.2	......	122.6
Rural	123.4	135.0	......	109.4
(2) Population of working age (16 to 59 years)	82.4	91.5	......	111.0
Including:				
Urban	17.7	21.9	......	123.7
Rural	64.7	69.6	......	107.6
(3) Number of persons working for hire (annual averages, including agriculture and forestry)	11.35	15.76	......	138.9
Of which:				
A. (a) In urban communities	7.0	9.7	......	138.6
(b) In rural communities	4.3	6.0	......	139.5
B. (a) In industry	3.5	4.6	......	131.4
(b) In building trades	0.6	1.9	......	316.7
(c) In transportation	1.3	1.5	......	115.4
(d) In social welfare and cultural organizations	1.1	1.6	......	145.5

II. *Capitalization at End of Year* (billions of rubles):				
(1) Basic capital:				
(a) At 1926–27 prices	69.8	126.9	......	182.0
(2) Operating capital:				
(a) At 1926–27 prices	15.0	34.5	......	230.0
(b) At prices of respective years	15.2	28.9	......	190.0
III. *Capital Investments* (billions of rubles):				
Total:				
(a) At 1926–27 prices	8.2	27.7	92.7	338.0
(b) At prices of respective years	8.0	19.6	74.2	245.0
Including:				
(1) Basic capital:				
(a) At 1926–27 prices	7.3	23.4	77.7	321.0
(b) At prices of respective years	7.1	17.1	64.6	241.0
(2) Operating capital:				
(a) At 1926–27 prices	0.93	4.27	15.0	459.0
(b) At prices of respective years	0.94	3.58	13.8	380.0
IV. *National Income* (net production in billions of rubles):				
(a) At 1926–27 prices	24.4	49.7	186.6	203.0
(b) At prices of respective years	24.7	43.3	175.1	175.0
V. *Electrification:*				
(1) Basic capital at end of year (in billions of rubles at 1926–27 prices; exclusive of power stations in industrial plants)	0.93	4.87	......	524.0
Of which, in central regional stations	0.71	3.66	......	516.0

	1927–28	1932–33	*Total for 5 Years*	*Ratio of* 1932–33 *to* 1927–28 *Per cent*
(2) Capital investments (in billions of rubles; exclusive of power stations in industrial plants):				
(a) At 1926–27 prices	0.31	1.44	4.47	465.0
(b) At prices of respective years	0.284	0.861	3.059	303.0
Of which, in central regional stations:				
(a) At 1926–27 prices	0.25	1.02	3.36	408.0
(b) At prices of respective years	0.230	0.605	2.302	263.0
(3) Total aggregate power capacity (thousands of kw.)	1,700.0	5,500.0	......	324.0
Exclusive of power stations in industrial plants	880.0	3,750.0	......	426.0
Central regional stations	520.0	3,100.0	......	596.0
(4) Output of electric power (billions of kw.-hours)	5.1	22.0	65.0	431.0
Exclusive of power stations in industrial plants	2.4	15.5	......	646.0
Central regional stations	1.9	14.0	......	737.0
VI. *Industry:*				
(1) Basic capital at end of year (in billions of rubles at 1926–27 prices), not including industrial housing	9.6	30.7	......	320.0
Same, exclusive of regional and municipal electric plants	8.6	25.8	......	300.0

Of which, in industries covered by the plan of the Supreme Council of National Economy	6.8	20.7	......	304.0
(2) Capital investments (in billions of rubles), not including industrial housing:				
(a) At 1926–27 prices	1.9	7.4	24.9	390.0
Same, exclusive of regional and municipal electric plants	1.6	6.0	20.4	375.0
Of which, in industries covered by the plan	1.3	4.9	16.4	377.0
(b) At prices of respective years	1.8	4.6	18.0	256.0
Same, exclusive of regional and municipal electric plants	1.5	3.8	14.9	253.0
Of which, in industries covered by the plan	1.2	3.0	12.1	250.0
(3) Number of workers (not including salaried employees) in census industry* (thousands)	2,750.0	3,631.0	......	132.0
Of which, in industries covered by the plan	2,103.0	2,806.0	......	133.0
(4) Gross production (in billions of rubles)				
A. All Industry:				
(a) At 1926–27 prices	18.3	43.2	154.6	236.0
(b) At prices of respective years	18.0	32.7	131.8	182.0
Including:				
Group A (Producers' goods)				
(a) At 1926–27 prices	6.0	18.1	60.1	302.0
(b) At prices of respective years	5.8	12.4	47.0	214.0
Group B (Consumers' goods)				
(a) At 1926–27 prices	12.3	25.1	94.5	204.0
(b) At prices of respective years	12.2	20.3	84.8	166.0

* See Appendix III

	1927–28	1932–33	*Total Years*	*Ratio of* 1932–33 *to* 1927–28 *Per cent*
B. Census Industry:				
Total				
(a) At 1926–27 prices	13.9	36.6	126.6	263.0
(b) At prices of respective years	13.5	27.1	105.8	201.0
Group A				
(a) At 1926–27 prices	5.6	17.4	57.3	311.0
(b) At prices of respective years	5.4	11.8	44.6	219.0
Group B				
(a) At 1926–27 prices	8.3	19.2	69.3	231.0
(b) At prices of respective years	8.1	15.3	61.2	189.0
C. Industry covered by the plan of the Supreme Council of National Economy:				
Total				
(a) At 1926–27 prices	10.9	30.4	103.8	279.0
(b) At prices of respective years	10.4	22.0	85.0	212.0
Group A				
(a) At 1926–27 prices	4.4	14.5	47.2	330.0
(b) At prices of respective years	4.2	9.8	36.4	233.0
Group B				
(a) At 1926–27 prices	6.5	15.9	56.6	245.0
(b) At prices of respective years	6.2	12.2	48.6	197.0

D. Small industries (including flour-milling):				
Total				
(a) At 1926–27 prices	4.4	6.6	28.0	150.0
(b) At prices of respective years	4.5	5.6	26.0	124.0
Group A				
(a) At 1926–27 prices	0.4	0.7	2.8	175.0
(b) At prices of respective years	0.4	0.6	2.4	150.0
Group B				
(a) At 1926–27 prices	4.0	5.9	25.2	148.0
(b) At prices of respective years	4.1	5.0	23.6	122.0
(5) Net production (billions of rubles):				
(a) At 1926–27 prices	6.6	16.3	57.7	248.0
(b) At prices of respective years	6.4	12.7	49.7	197.0
Same, including excise taxes	7.8	14.8	59.0	190.0
(6) Gross production, marketable portion (billions of rubles):				
Total				
(a) At 1926–27 prices	15.8	38.2	135.1	242.0
(b) At prices of respective years	15.5	29.0	115.3	187.0
Of which, industries covered by the plan	8.4	18.8	70.8	224.0
Group A				
(a) At 1926–27 prices	5.2	16.5	53.6	317.0
(b) At prices of respective years	5.0	11.3	41.9	226.0
Of which, industries covered by the plan	3.5	8.8	31.8	251.0
Group B				
(a) At 1926–27 prices	10.6	21.7	81.5	205.0
(b) At prices of respective years	10.5	17.7	73.4	169.0
Of which, industries covered by the plan	4.9	10.0	39.0	204.0

	1927–28	1932–33	Total for 5 Years	Ratio of 1932–33 to 1927–28 Per cent
VII. *Agriculture* (billions of rubles):				
(1) Basic capital at end of year (invested in agriculture proper, excluding fishing, hunting and forestry)				
At 1926–27 prices	28.7	38.9	......	136.0
Of which, machines and implements	3.3	6.4	......	194.0
(2) Capital investments (in agriculture proper)				
(a) At 1926–27 prices	3.1	4.9	20.6	158.0
Same, exclusive of buildings	1.7	3.3	12.9	194.0
(b) At prices of respectiye years	3.0	4.3	19.0	143.0
Same, exclusive of buildings	1.7	3.0	12.3	177.0
(3) Gross production (for agricultural years):				
(a) At 1926–27 prices	16.7	25.8	105.7	155.0
(b) At prices of respective years	17.4	26.1	111.1	150.0
Of which, in agriculture proper, including animals raised:				
(a) At 1926–27 prices	14.5	22.6	92.0	156.0
Same, not including animals raised	14.0	21.6	87.9	154.0
A. Crops, total	9.2	14.5	58.7	158.0
Of which: grain crops	3.7	5.6	23.3	151.0
Of which: industrial crops	0.91	1.85	6.9	203.0
B. Animal products	5.3	8.1	33.3	153.0
Same, not including animals raised	4.8	7.1	29.2	150.0

(b) At prices of respective years	15.4	23.2	99.1	151.0
Same, not including animals raised	14.9	22.2	95.0	149.0
A. Crops, total	10.0	15.3	65.6	153.0
Of which: grain crops	4.0	6.1	26.9	153.0
Of which: industrial crops	0.97	1.81	7.4	187.0
B. Animal products	5.4	7.9	33.5	146.0
Same, not including animals raised	4.9	6.9	29.4	141.0
(4) Net production (for agricultural years):				
(a) At 1926–27 prices	10.8	16.7	68.4	155.0
(b) At prices of respective years	11.3	16.7	71.8	148.0
Of which in agriculture proper:				
(a) At 1926–27 prices	8.9	13.8	56.1	156.0
(b) At prices of respective years	9.5	14.2	60.6	150.0
(5) Gross production, marketable portion (for agricultural years):				
A. Not including purchases by peasants:				
(a) At 1926–27 prices	3.8	7.9	28.5	208.0
(b) At prices of respective years	3.9	7.5	28.6	192.0
Of which, in agriculture proper:				
(a) At 1926–27 prices, total	2.9	6.4	22.0	221.0
(1) Crops, total	1.43	3.47	11.7	243.0
Of which: grain crops	0.45	1.14	3.7	253.0
Of which: industrial crops	0.60	1.56	5.3	260.0
(2) Animal products	1.47	2.89	10.3	197.0
(b) At prices of respective years	3.0	6.2	22.8	207.0
(1) Crops, total	1.55	3.54	12.7	228.0
Of which: grain crops	0.48	1.23	4.2	256.0
Of which: industrial crops	0.64	1.49	5.6	233.0

	1927–28	1932–33	*Total for 5 Years*	*Ratio of* 1932–33 *to* 1927–28 *Per cent*
(2) Animal products	1.47	2.69	10.1	183.0
B. In addition, purchases by peasants:				
(a) At 1926–27 prices	2.8	4.5	17.8	161.0
(b) At prices of respective years	2.9	4.4	18,5	152.0
C. Total marketable portion of agricultural production:				
(a) At 1926–27 prices	6.6	12.4	46.3	188.0
(b) At prices of respective years	6.8	11.9	47.1	175.0
VIII. *Transportation:*				
(1) Basic capital (billions of rubles at 1926–27 prices)	12.3	23.3	......	189.0
Of which, in railways	10.8	18.2	......	169.0
(2) Capital investments (billions of rubles):				
(a) At 1926–27 prices	0.95	4.65	13.64	489.0
(b) At prices of respective years	0.90	3.11	10.00	346.0
(3) Of which, investments in railways:				
(a) At 1926–27 prices	0.76	3.08	9.52	405.0
(b) At prices of respective years	0.71	1.90	6.71	266.0
(4) Railway freight traffic (billions of ton—kilometers)	88.1	162.7	......	185.0
(5) Gross revenue of railways (billions of rubles)	1.6	3.1	12.1	194.0

IX. *Construction:*				
(1) Buildings and structures, exclusive of farm construction (billions of rubles):				
(a) At 1926–27 prices	2.6	12.5	38.7	481.0
(b) At prices of respective years	2.5	7.4	26.5	296.0
(2) Same, including farm construction:				
(a) At 1926–27 prices	3.9	13.7	45.0	351.0
(b) At prices of respective years	3.8	8.6	32.7	226.0
X. *Budget and Currency Circulation* (billions of rubles):				
(1) Central budget, gross	6.8	14.1	53.9	207.0
(2) Central budget, net	4.2	9.6	35.9	229.0
(3) Local budgets	1.7	4.1	15.1	241.0
(4) Total, net	5.9	13.7	51.0	233.0
(5) Money in circulation (at end of year)	1.97	3.22	......	163.0
XI. *Financing of the National Economy and of Social Welfare and Cultural Organizations by Financial Institutions of the Soviet Union* (billions of rubles):				
Total	9.46	23.07	86.01	244.0
Including:				
(1) General administration and national defense	1.64	2.31	9.98	141.0
(2) Social welfare and cultural organizations	2.40	5.88	21.40	245.0
(3) National economy	5.42	14.88	54.63	275.0
Including: Industry	1.91	4.47	17.83	234.0
Including: Agriculture proper	0.70	1.87	6.75	268.0
Including: Transportation	0.86	2.79	9.47	324.0

	1927–28	1932–33	*Total for 5 Years*	*Ratio of 1932–33 to 1927–28 Per cent*
XII. *Price Indexes:*				
(1) Producers' prices (1926–27 = 1,000):				
(a) General index of industrial prices (selling prices of state industries)	961.0	731.0	......	76.1
Group A (producers' goods)	966.0	677.0	......	70.1
Group B (consumers' goods)	957.0	782.0	......	81.7
(b) General index of agricultural prices (purchasing prices of state procuring agencies)	1,047.0	991.0	......	94.6
Grain	1,071.0	1,122.0	......	104.8
Industrial crops	1,070.0	967.0	......	90.4
Animal products	1,014.0	937.0	......	92.4
(2) Wholesale price index of the Central Statistical Board (1913 = 1,000)	1,782.0	1,469.0	......	82.4
(a) Agricultural prices	1,565.0	1,502.0	......	96.0
(b) Industrial prices	1,877.0	1,445.0	......	77.0
(3) Retail price index of the Central Statistical Board, (1913 = 1,000)	2,070.0	1,610.0	......	77.8
(a) Agricultural prices	2,090.0	1,660.0	......	79.4
(b) Industrial prices	2,050.0	1,580.0	......	77.1

(4) Index of cost of living of the Central Bureau of Labor Statistics (1913 = 1,000):				
All articles	2,050.0	1,760.0	......	85.9
Articles purchased or rented	2,173.0	1,782.0	......	82.0
(5) Index of construction costs, with allowance for rationalization (1926–27 = 1,000):				
All construction	961.0	564.0	......	58.7
(a) Industrial construction	957.0	506.0	......	52.9
(b) Railway construction	972.0	641.0	......	65.9
(c) Housing construction	943.0	536.0	......	56.8

TABLE II

STRUCTURE OF NATIONAL ECONOMY OF THE SOVIET UNION UNDER THE FIVE-YEAR PLAN

	1927–28	1932–33	Ratio of 1932–33 to 1928–29 Per cent
I. *Power:*			
A. Human labor:			
(1) Number of persons of working age per 100 of population	54.2	54.1	99.8
(2) Number of persons working for hire, per 100 of population of working age	13.8	17.2	124.6
(3) Same, in urban communities	38.7	42.3	109.3
(4) Number of persons not engaged in work, per 100 of population of working age in urban communities	6.4	2.4	37.5
(5) Number of persons occupied in the several fields, per 100 of total number of persons working for hire (exclusive of agricultural laborers):			
(a) Industry	37.7	35.7	94.7
Of which: large-scale industry	33.3	31.6	94.9
(b) Transportation	15.3	12.0	78.4
Of which: railway transportation	10.8	7.8	72.2
(c) Construction	6.8	14.6	214.7
(d) Social welfare and cultural activities	12.1	12.0	99.2

(6) Number per 100 industrial workers in industries covered by the plan of the Supreme Council of national Economy:			
(a) Skilled workers	41.3	62.0	150.1
(b) Technicians	0.6	1.6	266.7
(c) Engineers	0.6	1.3	216.7
(7) Index of working hours (per cent of pre-war)	77.0	70.5	91.6
(8) District agronomists per 100,000 of rural population	4.5	9.3	206.7
B. Mechanical and electrical power equipment (KW-hours, per 1 man-hour):			
(9) In industry	1.24	2.61	210.5
(10) In transportation	2.05	3.11	151.7
C. Power and fuel consumption:			
(11) Distribution of power consumed by nature of power (per cent of total)			
(a) Mechanical including electric	42.0	61.9	147.4
Of which: electric	15.4	37.4	242.8
Animal	58.0	38.1	65.7
(12) Distribution of fuel consumed by nature of fuel (per cent of total, estimated in standard fuel units)			
(a) Solid mineral fuels	59.4	65.3	109.9
(b) Petroleum products	18.2	16.2	89.0
(c) Peat	4.8	7.1	147.9
(d) Wood	17.6	11.4	64.8
(13) Share of electric power production in total fuel consumption (per cent of total)	9.5	21.0	221.1

	1927–28	1932–33	*Ratio of 1932–33 to 1928–29 Per cent*
II. *Welfare and Cultural Status of the Population:*			
A. Real income (allowing for decrease in prices), rubles per person a year:			
(1) Non-agricultural population:			
(a) Total	313.8	537.8	171.4
(b) Persons working for hire	366.4	647.7	176.8
(2) Agricultural population:			
(a) Total	116.8	195.5	167.4
(b) Persons on individual farms	116.6	188.7	161.8
(c) Persons on collective farms	132.7	243.2	183.2
(3) Index of real wages of workers in industry (1913=100)	122.5	208.9	170.5
B. Cultural status and general living conditions:			
(1) Literacy:			
A. Number of literate persons, per 100 of population, 8 years of age and above:			
(a) Urban	78.5	86.7	110.4
(b) Rural	48.3	74.6	154.5
(c) Total population	53.9	77.0	142.9
B. Number of children attending school, per 100 of children of school age:			
(a) In urban communities	100.0	100.0	100.0
(b) In rural communities	79.3	92.4	116.5

(2) Public health. Number of hospital beds, per 10,000 of population:			
(a) In urban communities	49.0	51.0	104.1
(b) In rural communities	5.0	6.0	120.0
(3) Housing conditions of urban population: dwelling space per person, in square meters:			
(a) For workers in industries covered by the plan of the S.C.N.E.	5.60	7.30	130.4
(b) For all workers in socialized sector of national economy	5.90	7.00	118.6
(c) For workers in private sector of national economy	5.55	5.70	102.7
(d) For urban population as a whole	5.70	6.30	110.5
(4) Food consumption:			
A. Annual consumption per person in urban communities:			
(a) Bread (centners)	1.79	1.79	100.0
(b) Meat (kilograms)	49.1	62.7	127.7
(c) Eggs (pieces)	90.7	155.0	170.9
(d) Dairy products (kilograms)	218.0	339.3	155.6
B. Annual consumption per person in rural communities:			
(a) Bread (centners)	2.21	2.34	105.9
(b) Meat (kilograms)	22.6	26.4	116.8
(c) Eggs (pieces)	49.6	72.0	145.2
(d) Dairy products (kilograms)	183.0	228.0	124.6

	1927–28	1932–33	*Ratio of* 1932–33 *to* 1928–29 *Per cent*
(5) Budget of worker's family, distribution of expenses (per cent of total budget):			
(a) Industrial products	34.2	32.5	95.0
(b) Agricultural products	43.2	39.0	90.3
(c) Dwelling	8.7	9.5	109.2
(d) Social and cultural needs	5.3	8.2	154.7
(e) Other expenses	3.6	4.8	133.3
(f) Savings	5.0	6.0	120.0
III. *Socialization and Cooperation:*			
(1) Gross production of socialized sector in proportion to total industrial and agricultural production (at constant prices) per cent	45.9	66.5	144.9
(2) Gross grain production in socialized sector in proportion to total grain production, per cent	2.1	15.8	752.4
Of which, share of collective farming, per cent	1.0	11.3	1,130.0
(3) Production of cooperative enterprises in small industry in proportion to total production of small industry, per cent	19.4	53.8	277.3
(4) Sales in cooperative retail trade, in proportion to total retail trade	60.2	78.9	131.1
(5) Proportion of basic capital invested in socialized sector of national economy (at constant prices), per cent	52.7	68.9	130.7
(6) Proportion of capital investments going into socialized sector of national economy (at constant prices), per cent	57.7	83.7	145.1

(7) Households belonging to cooperative associations in proportion to total households in agriculture, per cent	37.5	85.0	226.7
(8) Membership of consumers' cooperatives in proportion to population, per cent:			
(a) In urban communities	45.3	70.0	154.5
(b) In rural communities	19.1	40.0	209.4
IV. *Industrialization:*			
(1) National income distribution by sources (at prices of respective years), per cent of total income:			
(a) Industry	31.6	34.2	108.2
(b) Construction	6.4	9.5	148.4
(c) Agriculture	45.8	38.7	84 5
(d) Transportation and communication	5.1	6.1	119.6
(e) Trade	11.1	11.5	103.6
(2) Distribution of basic capital at end of year, per cent of total:			
(a) Industry (including industrial housing)	14.0	22.9	163.6
(b) Agriculture	41.0	30.4	74.1
(c) Electrification	1.4	4.3	307.1
(d) Transportation	16.6	17.2	103.6
(e) Housing (not including industrial)	17.2	11.9	69.2
(f) Other	9.8	13.3	135.7
(3) Distribution of capital investments, per cent of total			
(a) Industry (including industrial housing)	23.7	26.2	110.5
(b) Agriculture	43.4	32.2	74.2
(c) Electrification	4.0	5.4	135.0
(d) Transportation	12.7	19.4	152.8
(e) Housing (urban, not including industrial housing)	7.2	6.7	93.1
(f) Other	9.0	10.1	112.2

	1927–28	1932–33	*Ratio of* 1932–33 *to* 1927–28 *Per cent*
(4) Distribution of gross production of industry covered by the plan, of the S.C.N.E., per cent of total:			
A. Production of producers' goods	40.3	47.8	118.6
Of which:			
Fuel	8.5	6.9	81.2
Metals	17.1	19.0	111.1
Chemical products	2.3	4.3	187.0
B. Production of consumers' goods	59.7	52.2	87.4
Of which: textiles	32.3	25.7	79.6
(5) Distribution of marketable portion of national production, per cent:			
(a) Industry	69.5	70.8	101.9
(b) Agriculture	30.5	29.2	95.7
V. *Technical Reconstruction and Rationalization:*			
(1) In industry			
A. Fuel consumption, tons:			
In coal industry, per 100 tons produced	7.8	6.6	84.6
In petroleum industry, per 100 tons produced	7.5	5.6	74.7
In metal industry, per 1,000 units of production, standard fuel units	6.2	4.4	71.0
In cotton industry, per 1,000 pieces of goods	10.69	7.96	74.5

B. Efficiency of equipment:			
Output of pig iron, per 1 blast furnace, thousands of tons...	85.0	123.0	144.7
Output of steel, per 1 open hearth furnace, thousands of tons.	25.7	31.4	122.2
Output of fabrics in textile industry:			
(a) Cotton:			
Kilograms of yarn, per 1,000 spindles in 8 working hours.	2,300.0	2,576.0	112.0
Meters of unbleached cloth, per 1 loom in 8 working hours	25.6	27.0	105.5
(b) Linen:			
Kilograms of yarn, per 1,000 spindles in 8 working hours.	5,740.0	7,450.0	129.8
Square meters of cotton, per 1 loom in 8 working hours...	35.9	38.0	105.8
C. General indicators:			
(1) Rate of consumption of:			
(a) Raw materials, industrial........................	100.0	72.0	72.0
(b) Raw materials, agricultural......................	100.0	82.0	82.0
(c) Fuel..	100.0	70.0	70.0
(2) Index of productivity of labor.......................	100.0	210.0	210.0
(3) Production costs....................................	100.0	65.0	65.0
(2) In agriculture:			
A. Per cent of planted area:			
(a) On which land demarcation will be completed at end of five-year period.....................................	....	80.6	......
(b) Which will at end of five-year period be provided with chemical fertilizers..................................	....	10.3	......
Of which:			
Area planted to grain..............................	....	6.5	......
Area planted to principal industrial crops............	....	89.0	......
(c) Provided with selected seeds........................	3.9	57.6	1,476.9

	1927–28	1932–33	Ratio of 1932–33 to 1928–29 Per cent
B. Yield in centners, per hectare:			
(a) Grain crops	7.6	9.5	125.0
(b) Cotton	9.3	12.5	134.4
(c) Flax-fiber	2.3	3.6	156.5
(3) In railway transportation:			
(a) Productivity of labor: thousands of ton-kilometers, per employee	115.2	201.1	174.6
(b) Locomotive-kilometers per 1,000,000 ton-kilometers of freight	4,200.0	3,292.0	78.4
(c) Cost of transportation, kopecks, per ton-kilometer	1.21	0.96	79.3
VI. *Distribution:*			
(1) Distribution of national income, per cent of total:			
(a) Non-agricultural population	42.7	42.7	100.0
Of which, proletariat	32.1	37.0	115.3
(b) Agricultural population	49.8	42.5	85.3
Of which, collective farming	0.5	5.3	1,060.0
(c) Socialized sector of national economy	7.5	14.8	197.3
(2) Total budget, central and local, net, distribution by general classes of revenues and expenditures, per cent, at prices of respective years):			
A. Revenues (per cent of total):			
(a) Taxes	59.0	53.4	90.5

Of which direct taxes	30.0	31.5	105.0
Of which, indirect taxes	29.0	21.9	75.5
(b) Non-tax revenue	15.7	17.4	110.8
(c) Loans	11.8	12.4	105.1
(d) All other	13.5	16.8	124.4
B. Expenditures, per cent of total:			
(a) Social welfare and cultural service	21.1	21.9	103.8
(b) Financing of national economy	41.1	51.1	124.3
(c) All other	37.8	27.0	71.4
(3) General financial plan; distribution of revenues and expenditures by general classes (per cent of total):			
A. Revenues from:			
(a) Government budget	55.9	50.6	90.5
Of which, central budget	37.1	32.7	88.1
(b) Credit system	9.1	7.9	86.8
(c) Social insurance	11.0	10.9	99.1
(d) Resources of economic organizations	17.8	22.5	126.4
(e) Outside sources	6.2	8.1	130.6
B. Expenditures for:			
(a) Economic activities	57.3	64.5	112.6
Of which:			
Agriculture	7.4	8.1	109.5
Industry	20.2	19.4	96.0
Electrification	2.9	3.6	124.1
Transportation	9.1	12.1	133.0
Housing construction	4.2	5.2	123.8
Other	13.5	16.1	119.3
(b) Social welfare and cultural activities	25.4	25.5	100.4
(c) General administration and defense	17.3	10.0	57.8

TABLE III

BASIC INDICATORS OF THE FIVE-YEAR PLAN OF NATIONAL ECONOMY AS COMPARED WITH 1913 AND WITH THE PRECEDING FIVE-YEAR PERIOD

	1913	1922–1923	1927–1928	1932–1933	Total for 5 Years		Ratio to 1913		
					1923–24 to 1927–28	1928–29 to 1932–33	1922–23 Per cent	1927–28 Per cent	1932–33 Per cent
I. *Population:*									
(a) Total number (millions):	139.7	133.3	151.3	169.2	143.8	162.0	95.4	108.3	121.1
Including:									
Urban	25.7	21.9	27.9	34.2	25.3	31.5	85.2	108.6	133.1
Rural	114.0	111.4	123.4	135.0	118.5	130.5	97.7	108.2	118.4
(b) Number of persons working for hire, total (thousands)	11,200.0	6,803.0	11,350.0	15,764.0	9,740.0	13,794.0	60.7	101.3	140.8
Of which, in census industry	2,900.0	1,706.0	3,072.0	4,080.0	2,550.0	3,626.0	58.8	105.9	140.7
II. *Electrification:*									
1. Capacity of primary motors in industrial plants (thousands of KW.)	960.0	.....	2,550.0	6,200.0	......	......	.....	265.6	645.8
2. Capacity of primary motors in public utility stations (thousands of KW.)	96.0	.....	880.0	3,750.0	......	......	.....	916.7	3,906.3
3. Output of electric energy (millions of KW.)	1,945.0	1,095.0	5,050.0	22,000.0	16,000.0	65,000.0	56.3	259.6	1,131.1
III. *Agriculture:*									
1. Planted area (millions of hectares)	116.7	80.0	115.6	142.0	105.0	129.0	70.4	101.7	124.9
Of which, planted to grain	102.7	70.0	97.2	112.0	84.0	104.0	68.2	94.8	109.2
Of which, planted to industrial crops	5.5	4.0	7.3	12.0	6.0	10.0	72.7	132.7	218.1
2. Live stock: bovine cattle or its equivalent (millions of heads):	85.0	65.0	85.0	114.0	77.0	......	76.8	100.0	134.1
Of which:									
(a) draft animals (millions of heads)	36.0	22.0	31.0	48.0	27.0	......	61.8	86.1	133.3
(b) breeding stock (millions of heads)	49.0	43.0	54.0	66.0	50.0	......	87.8	110.2	134.7

3. Production (physical volume):									
(a) Grain (millions of tons)	81.2	61.0	73.7	106.0	335.0	445.0	75.1	89.5	130.5
(b) Cotton (thousands of tons)	744.0	28.0	719.0	1,907.0	2,369.0	6,857.0	3.7	96.6	256.4
(c) Flax fiber (thousands of tons)	454.0	306.0	292.0	621.0	1,501.0	2,210.0	67.4	63.8	136.8
(d) Sugar beet (millions of tons)	10.9	2.0	10.1	20.0	31.0	74.0	18.3	92.7	183.5
(e) Oil seeds (thousands of tons)	2,554.0	2,098.0	3,401.0	6,721.0	14,257.0	25,275.0	82.1	133.2	263.2
4. Production at pre-war prices (billions of rubles)	10.5	7.8	11.0	17.0	49.6	......	74.3	104.8	161.9
5. Marketable portion of grain production (millions of tons)	20.4	.....	8.0	19.6	44.0	65.0	.....	39.2	96.1
IV. *Industry:*									
1. Production, physical volume:									
A. Producers' goods									
(a) Coal (millions of tons)	28.9	11.0	35.4	75.0	125.0	279.0	38.1	122.5	259.5
(b) Petroleum (millions of tons)	9.3	5.0	11.6	22.0	44.0	86.0	53.8	124.7	236.6
(c) Peat (millions of tons)	1.6	3.0	6.9	16.0	24.0	57.0	187.5	431.3	1,000.0
(d) Iron ore (millions of tons)	9.2	.....	5.7	19.0	17.0	64.0	4.3	62.0	206.5
(e) Pig iron (millions of tons)	4.2	.....	3.3	10.0	10.0	33.0	7.1	78.6	238.1
(f) Steel ingots, open hearth (millions of tons)	4.2	.....	4.0	10.4	13.0	35.0	11.9	95.2	247.6
(g) Rolled steel (millions of tons)	3.5	.5	3.2	8.0	10.0	27.0	14.3	91.4	228.6
(h) Agricultural machinery (millions of rubles at pre-war prices)	67.0	14.0	125.0	498.0	286.0	......	20.9	186.6	743.3
(i) Cement (millions of barrels)	12.3	1.0	11.9	41.0	37.0	135.0	8.1	96.7	333.3
(j) Bricks (millions of pieces)	2,144.0	213.0	1,785.0	9,300.0	5,178.0	29,750.0	9.9	83.3	433.8
(k) Superphosphates (thousands of tons)	55.0	5.0	150.0	3,400.0	379.0	7,291.0	9.1	272.7	6,181.8
(l) Sulphuric acid (thousands of tons)	150.0	35.0	208.0	1,450.0	674.0	3,801.0	23.3	138.7	966.7
B. Consumers' goods:									
(a) Cotton yarn (thousands of tons)	271.0	75.0	328.0	620.0	1,148.0	2,367.0	27.7	121.0	228.8
(b) Wool cloth (millions of meters)	95.0	22.0	97.0	270.0	328.0	849.0	23.2	102.1	284.2
(c) Linen cloth (millions of square meters)	......	93.0	165.0	500.0	728.0	1,537.0	.....	.....	.....

NOTE: Figures in columns 6 and 7 referring to population, planted areas, number of live stock, and transportation are five-year averages.

	1913	1922–1923	1927–1928	1932–1933	Total for 5 Years: 1923–24 to 1927–28	Total for 5 Years: 1928–29 to 1932–33	Ratio to 1913: 1922–23 Per cent	Ratio to 1913: 1927–28 Per cent	Ratio to 1913: 1932–33 Per cent
(d) Sugar, granulated (thousands of tons)	1,290.0*	211.0	1,340.0	2,600.0	4,124.0	9,640.0	16.4	103.9	201.6
(e) Salt (thousands of tons)	1,978.0	950.0	2,300.0	3,250.0	8,269.0	14,473.0	48.0	116.3	164.3
(f) Rubber shoes (millions of pairs)	28.0	10.0	37.0	75.0	113.0	274.0	35.7	132.1	267.9
2. Production of census industry, at pre-war prices (billions of rubles)	6.4	2.0	8.1	21.0	......	......	31.3	126.6	328.1
3. Real wages of industrial workers, including rent and other municipal services (per cent of 1913)	100.0	54.2	122.5	208.9	......	......	54.2	122.5	208.9
V. *Transportation:*									
1. Mileage in operation (thousands of km.)	59.0	71.0	77.0	90.0	75.0	82.0	120.3	130.5	152.5
2. Freight traffic (in millions of tons)	132.0	58.0	151.0	281.0	111.0	217.0	44.3	114.4	212.9
Of which:									
Grain	18.0	9.0	14.0	25.0	13.0	19.0	50.0	77.8	138.9
Coal	26.0	8.0	30.0	58.0	21.0	45.0	30.8	115.4	223.1
VI. *National income* (billions of rubles):									
At pre-war prices	14.0	7.0	15.0	30.0	63.0	115.0	50.0	107.1	214.3
At prices of respective years	......	7.0	25.0	43.0	......	175.0	.....	.....	.....

* 1914 production.

TABLE IV

PROGRESS OF SOCIALIZATION

	Proportion of socialized sector and of private sector in national economy, per cent of total.			
	Socialized Sector			*Private Sector*
	State	*Co-operative*	*Total*	
1. *Number of persons occupied:*				
1927–28	15.1	3.2	18.3	81.7
1932–33	16.3	14.4	30.7	69.3
2. *Number of persons working for hire:*				
1927–28	70.5	9.4	79.9	20.1
1932–33	70.7	13.2	83.9	16.1
Of which:				
(a) Industry:				
1927–28	85.7	5.7	91.4	8.6
1932–33	86.9	6.5	93.4	6.6
(b) Agriculture:				
1927–28	28.6	4.7	33.3	67.7
1932–33	34.5	6.9	41.4	58.6
3. *Capital investments:*				
1927–28	53.9	3.8	57.7	42.3
1932–33	74.4	9.3	83.7	16.3
Of which:				
(a) Industry:				
1927–28	94.4	1.8	96.2	3.8
1932–33	96.2	2.5	98.7	1.3
(b) Agriculture:				
1927–28	2.6	5.2	7.8	92.2
1932–33	7.0	24.4	31.4	68.6
4. *Capital at end of year:*				
A. Basic capital:				
1927–28	51.0	1.7	52.7	47.3
1932–33	63.6	5.3	68.9	31.1

	Proportion of socialized sector and of private sector in national economy, per cent of total.			
	Socialized Sector			Private Sector
	State	Co-operative	Total	
Of which:				
(a) Industry:				
1927–28	89.2	3.0	92.2	7.8
1932–33	94.5	2.3	96.8	3.2
(b) Agriculture:				
1927–28	2.7	2.2	4.9	95.1
1932–33	4.9	9.4	14.3	85.7
B. Operating capital:				
1927–28	41.5	14.9	56.4	43.6
1932–33	39.5	28.8	68.3	31.7
Of which:				
(a) Industry:				
1927–28	87.3	11.9	99.2	0.8
1932–33	74.3	25.4	99.7	0.3
(b) Agriculture:				
1927–28	2.7	1.5	4.2	95.8
1932–33	5.1	15.9	21.0	79.0
5. *Gross production:*				
1927–28	39.8	6.1	45.9	54.1
1932–33	52.7	13.8	66.5	33.5
Of which:				
(a) Census industry:				
1927–28	90.9	7.4	98.3	1.7
1932–33	91.1	7.9	99.0	1.0
(b) Small scale industry:				
1927–28	1.3	19.4	20.7	79.3
1932–33	1.8	53.8	55.6	44.4
(c) All industry:				
1927–28	69.2	10.3	79.5	20.5
1932–33	77.5	14.9	92.4	7.6
B. Agriculture:				
1927–28	1.2	0.6	1.8	98.2
1932–33	3.2	11.5	14.7	85.3

	Proportion of socialized sector and of private sector in national economy, per cent of total.			
	Socialized Sector			*Private Sector*
	State	*Co-operative*	*Total*	
6. *Marketable portion of production:*				
1927–28	56.4	9.7	66.1	33.9
1932–33	65.8	16.0	81.8	18.2
Of which:				
A. Industry				
(a) Census industry:				
1927–28	89.7	8.4	98.1	1.9
1932–33	90.3	8.6	98.9	1.1
(b) Small scale industry:				
1927–28	1.4	19.3	20.7	79.3
1932–33	1.8	53.8	55.6	44.4
(c) All industry:				
1927–28	66.1	11.3	77.4	22.6
1932–33	75.8	16.0	91.8	8.2
B. Agriculture:				
1927–28	3.6	0.8	4.4	95.6
1932–33	8.6	16.7	25.3	74.7
7. *Commercial turnover:*				
1927–28	37.6	48.5	86.1	13.9
1932–33	36.9	59.9	96.8	3.2
Of which, retail trade:				
1927–28	14.8	60.2	75.0	25.0
1932–33	12.2	78.9	91.1	8.9
8. *National income:*				
1927–28	42.8	9.9	52.7	47.3
1932–33	48.4	17.9	66.3	33.7
Of which:				
(a) Industry:				
1927–28	78.7	8.4	87.1	12.9
1932–33	83.5	11.4	94.9	5.1
(b) Agriculture:				
1927–28	1.2	0.7	1.9	98.1
1932–33	3.1	11.8	14.9	85.1

TABLE V

PROGRESS OF COOPERATIVE ORGANIZATION

	1927–28	1932–33	*Ratio of* 1932–33 *to* 1927–28 *Per cent*
1. *Number of shareholders* (thousands):			
(a) Agricultural cooperation*	9,500	23,580	248.
Of which, in collective farming*	400	3,580	895.
(b) Artisans' associations	870	3,686	424.
(c) Consumers' societies:			
In urban communities	8,705	16,450	189.
In rural communities	13,876	31,800	229.
(d) Housing construction societies	247	875	354.
(e) House renting associations	963	......	.....
2. *Relative extent of cooperative organization:* †			
(a) Agricultural cooperation	37.5	85.0	227.0
(b) Artisans' associations	21.0	56.0	267.0
(c) Consumers' societies, urban	45.3	70.0	155.0
(d) Consumers' societies, rural	19.1	40.0	209.0
3. *Total amount of share capital* (millions of rubles):	334.6	2,590.0	774.0
Of which:			
(a) Agricultural cooperation	65.0	583.0	897.0
(b) Artisans' associations	43.0	366.0	851.0
(c) Consumers' societies:			
Urban	90.6	658.0	726.0
Rural	103.0	795.0	772.0
(d) Housing construction societies	30.0	188.0	627.0
(e) House renting associations	3.0	31.0	1,033.0
4. *Average value of share* (rubles):			
(a) Agricultural cooperation	6.85	24.70	361.0
(b) Artisans' associations	49.40	99.10	201.0
(c) Consumers' societies:			
Urban	10.40	40.00	385.0
Rural	7.42	25.00	337.0
(d) Housing construction societies	121.00	......	.....
(e) House renting associations	5.20	......	.....

* Numbers of households affiliated with cooperative organizations, in thousands.

† The relative extent of cooperative organizations is expressed, for agricultural cooperation, in percentages of the total number of households; for consumers' societies, in percentages of the adult population, urban and rural, respectively; for artisans' associations, in percentages of the total number of artisans.

TABLE VI

CAPITAL INVESTMENTS IN BASIC CAPITAL OF THE NATIONAL ECONOMY OF THE SOVIET UNION

(At prices of respective years)

	Amounts in Millions of Rubles			*Ratio of 1932–33 to 1927–28 per cent*	*Per Cent of Total*		
	1927–28	1932–33	*Total for 5 years*		1927–28	1932–33	*Total for 5 years*
I. *Industry* (Including industrial housing):	1,672	4,170	16,353	249.4	23.7	26.2	27.1
Of which, in regulated industry.........	1,318	3,465	13,500	262.9	18.7	21.7	22.3
Group A (producers' goods)...........	938	2,396	9,788	255.4	13.3	15.0	16.2
Group B (consumers' goods)..........	365	734	2,860	201.1	5.2	4.6	4.7
II. *Agriculture* (Land cultivation):							
(a) Including land organization and other measures of public policy....	3,084	5,516	23,152	178.8	43.4*	32.2*	35.8*
(b) Not including land organization and other measures of public policy....	3,022	4,341	18,998	143.6	42.8	27.2	31.4
Of which, machinery and implements	550	1,196	4,507	217.5	7.8	7.5	7.5
III. *Forestry*..........................	12	64	229	533.3	0.2	0.4	0.4

* Percentages of total (a) *i.e.*, including land organisation and other measures of public policy.

	Amounts in Millions of Rubles			*Ratio of 1932–33 to 1927–28 per cent*	*Per Cent of Total*		
	1927–28	1932–33	*Total for 5 years*		1927–28	1932–33	*Total for 5 years*
IV. *Electrification:*							
(a) Not including power stations in industrial plants	284	861	3,059	303.2	4.0	5.4	5.1
(b) Including power stations in industrial plants	349	1,061	3,844	304.0	5.0	6.6	6.4
Of which, central regional plants	230	605	2,302	263.0	3.3	3.8	3.8
V. *Transportation*	896	3,105	10,002	346.5	12.7	19.4	16.5
Of which, railway transportation	714	1,898	6,713	265.8	10.1	11.9	11.1
VI. *Posts, Telegraph, Telephone and Radio*	35	65	307	185.7	0.5	0.4	0.5
VII. *Trade and warehousing*	176	605	2,164	343.8	2.5	3.8	3.6
VIII. *Public education*	114	645	2,017	565.8	1.6	4.0	3.3
IX. *Health service*	89	227	778	255.1	1.3	1.4	1.3
X. *General administration*	67	91	413	135.8	1.0	0.6	0.7
XI. *Municipal enterprises*	174	725	2,233	416.7	2.5	4.5	3.7

XII. *Housing construction in urban communities:*							
(a) Including housing for requirements of industry, transportation, and electrification	711	1,647	5,885	231.6	10.1	10.3	9.7
(b) Not including housing for requirements of industry, transportation, and electrification	509	1,068	3,895	209.8	7.2	6.7	6.4
Total:							
(a) Including investments for land organization and other measures of public policy in agriculture	7,112	17,142	64,601	241.0	.....	.....	.....
(b) Not including measures of public policy in agriculture	7,050	15,967	60,447	226.5	100.0	100.0	100.0
Distribution by socialized and private fields:							
State	3,613	10,472	37,463	289.8	51.2	65.6	62.0
Cooperative	385	2,097	6,725	544.7	5.5	13.1	11.1
Private	3,052	3,398	16,259	111.3	43.3	21.3	26.9

TABLE VII

BASIC CAPITAL AND CAPITAL INVESTMENTS IN THE NATIONAL ECONOMY OF THE SOVIET UNION

	Amounts in Millions of Rubles (at 1925–26 prices)				*Ratio of basic capital on Oct. 1, 1933 to that on Oct. 1, 1928. Per cent*	*Distribution of basic capital. Per cent of Total*	
	Basic capital as on Oct. 1, 1928	*Depreciation in 5 years*	*Investments in 5 years*	*Basic capital on Oct. 1, 1933*		*Oct. 1, 1928*	*Oct. 1, 1933*
I. *Industry:* Including industrial housing	9,813	3,444	22,746	29,115	296.7	14.0	22.9
Of which, in regulated industry	7,940	2,762	18,808	23,986	302.1	11.3	18.8
Group A (producers' goods)	4,550	1,745	13,589	16,394	360.3	6.5	12.8
Group B (consumers' goods)	3,298	992	3,986	6,292	190.8	4.7	4.9
II. *Agriculture proper*	28,741	10,571	20,717	38,887	135.3	41.0	30.4
Of which, in agricultural implements and machinery	3,280	1,933	5,060	6,407	195.3	4.7	5.0
III. *Electrification:* Not including electric power stations at industrial plants	1,011	576	4,874	5,309	525.1	1.4	4.3
Of which, in central regional plants	769	446	3,667	3,990	518.9	1.1	3.1

IV. *Transportation*	11,653	2,546	12,905	22,012	188.9	16.6	17.2
Of which, in railway transportation	10,131	2,066	8,899	16,964	167.4	14.4	13.3
V. *Posts, Telegraph, Telephone and Radio*	286	101	416	601	210.1	0.4	0.5
VI. *Trade and warehousing*	701	379	3,195	3,517	501.7	1.0	2.7
VII. *Public education*	1,974	214	3,184	4,944	250.5	2.8	3.9
VIII. *Health service*	1,074	114	1,271	2,231	207.7	1.5	1.7
IX. *General administration*	656	116	657	1,197	182.5	0.9	0.9
X. *Municipal enterprises*	2,274	606	3,047	4,715	207.3	3.2	3.7
XI. *Housing construction in urban centers:*							
Including industrial housing	13,136	2,301	7,684	18,519	141.0	18.7	14.5
Not including industrial housing	11,971	2,062	5,342	15,251	127.4	17.2	11.9
TOTAL	70,154	20,729	78,354	127,779	182.2	100.0	100.0
Distribution by socialized and private sectors:							
State	35,786	8,922	54,347	81,211	226.9	51.0	63.6
Cooperative	1,198	869	6,449	6,778	565.8	1.7	5.3
Private	33,170	10,939	17,559	39,790	120.0	47.3	31.1
Distribution by economic functions:							
Production	27,567	11,734	41,068	56,901	206.4	39.3	44.5
Distribution	12,640	3,025	16,516	26,131	206.7	18.0	20.5
Consumption	29,947	5,969	20,769	44,747	149.4	42.7	35.0

NOTE: All figures in this table relating to basic capital have been calculated at 1925–26 prices, in order to make a comparison possible with the figures for previous years; as compared with the latter, greater precision has been introduced into the figures for capital in agriculture and in transportation.

TABLE VIII

NATIONAL INCOME OF THE SOVIET UNION
(Net production)

	Amounts in Millions of Rubles			*Ratio of 1932–33 to 1927–28 per cent*	*Per Cent of Total*		
	1927–28	1932–33	*For 5 years*		1927–28	1932–33	*For 5 years*
A. *At prices of respective years:*							
1. Agriculture	11,285	16,742	71,836	148.4	45.8	38.7	41.0
Same, exclusive of fishing, hunting, and forestry	9,466	14,159	60,558	149.6	38.4	32.7	34.6
2. Industry, including excise taxes	7,809	14,815	58,990	189.7	31.6	34.2	33.7
Industry, not including excise taxes	6,449	12,725	49,680	197.3	26.1	29.4	28.4
Of which, large scale industry (not including excise)	5,214	11,072	42,120	212.3	21.1	25.6	24.1
3. Construction	1,588	4,096	15,007	257.9	6.4	9.5	8.6
4. Transportation and Communication	1,261	2,620	9,630	207.8	5.1	6.1	5.5
Of which, railway transportation	1,061	2,294	8,302	216.2	4.3	5.3	4.7
5. Commerce	2,738	4,997	19,654	182.5	11.1	11.5	11.2
TOTAL	24,681	43,270	175,117	175.3	100.0	100.0	100.0

B. *At 1926–27 prices:*							
1. Agriculture	10,783	16,681	68,448	154.7	44.1	33.6	36.7
Same, exclusive of hunting, fishing, and forestry	8,868	13,827	56,091	155.9	36.3	27.8	30.1
2. Industry, including excise taxes	7,978	18,983	68,392	237.9	32.7	38.2	36.7
Industry, not including excise taxes	6,582	16,314	57,694	247.9	26.9	32.8	30.9
Of which, large scale industry (not including excise)	5,349	14,328	49,495	267.9	21.9	28.8	26.5
3. Construction	1,667	5,877	19,483	352.5	6.8	11.8	10.4
4. Transportation and Communication	1,176	2,191	8,293	186.3	4.8	4.4	4.4
Of which, railway transportation	982	1,907	7,091	194.2	4.0	3.8	3.8
5. Commerce	2,825	5,958	21,960	210.9	11.6	12.0	11.8
TOTAL	24,429	49,690	186,576	203.4	100.0	100.0	100.0

NOTE: The total national income for 1927–28, as shown in this table, is 900 million rubles lower than is shown in the "Control Figures for National Economy for 1928–29"; the difference is accounted for chiefly by that in the respective figures for agriculture which is due to greater precision in the calculation of goods consumed in production.

TABLE IX

PLAN OF FINANCING OF THE NATIONAL ECONOMY OF THE SOVIET UNION

(Net, exclusive of inter-departmental movement of funds)

	Amount in Millions of Rubles			*Ratio of 1932–33 to 1927–28 per cent*	*Per Cent of Total*		
	1927–28	1932–33	*For 5 years*		1927–28	1932–33	*For 5 years*
A. *Expenditures for:*							
1. Economic activities	5,422	14,881	54,629	274.5	57.3	64.5	63.5
Of which:							
(a) Industry	1,909	4,468	17,830	234.0	20.2	19.4	20.7
(b) Agriculture	698	1,873	6,746	268.3	7.4	8.1	7.8
(c) Electrical development	276	837	2,960	303.3	2.9	3.6	3.4
(d) Transportation	861	2,790	9,471	324.0	9.1	12.1	11.0
(e) Housing construction	400	1,190	4,028	297.5	4.2	5.2	4.7
2. Social welfare and cultural activities	2,400	5,884	21,396	245.2	25.4	25.5	24.9
Of which:							
Public education	1,029	2,995	10,385	291.1	10.9	13.0	12.1
3. General administration and defense	1,642	2,308	9,980	140.6	17.3	10.0	11.6
TOTAL	9,464	23,073	86,005	243.8	100.0	100.0	100.0

B. *Revenues from:*							
1. Government budgets	5,293	11,674	44,709	220.6	55.9	50.6	52.0
Of which: central budget	3,514	7,547	29,639	214.8	37.1	32.7	34.5
2. Credit system	861	1,822	6,628	211.6	9.1	7.9	7.7
3. Social insurance	1,039	2,524	9,180	242.9	11.0	10.9	10.7
4. Resources of economic organizations	1,680	5,201	18,961	309.6	17.8	22.5	22.0
5. Outside sources	591	1,852	6,527	313.4	6.2	8.1	7.6
TOTAL	9,464	23,073	86,005	243.8	100.0	100.0	100.0

TABLE X

ANNUAL DEVELOPMENTS UNDER THE FIVE-YEAR PLAN

	Amounts in Millions of Rubles							*Ratio of Each Year to Preceding Year, Per Cent*					*Ratio of*
	1927-28	1928-29	1929-30	1930-31	1931-32	1932-33	*For 5 Years*	1928-29 *to* 1927-28	1929-30 *to* 1928-29	1930-31 *to* 1929-30	1931-32 *to* 1930-31	1932-33 *to* 1931-32	1932-33 *to* 1927-28
I. Gross production of industry, at 1926–27 prices	18,312	21,164	25,009	29,643	35,584	43,196	154,596	115.6	118.2	118.5	120.0	121.4	236.0
Of which, industries covered by plan of the Supreme Council of National Economy	10,909	13.247	16,090	19,649	24,320	30,447	103,753	121.4	121.5	122.1	123.8	125.2	279.0
II. Gross production of agriculture, at 1926-27 prices	16,659	17,367	18,845	20,804	22,897	25,806	105,719	104.2	108.5	110.4	110.1	112.7	155.0
Of which, agriculture proper	14,526	15,038	16,304	18,054	19,935	22,630	91,961	103.5	108.4	110.7	110.4	113.5	155.8
III. National income (net production):													
(a) At 1926–27 prices	24,429	27,149	31,289	36,294	42,154	49,690	186,576	111.1	115.2	116.0	116.1	117.9	203.4
(b) At prices of respective years	24,681	27,385	30,884	34,829	38,749	43,270	175,117	111.0	112.8	112.8	111.3	111.7	175.3
IV. Capital investments (at prices of respective years)	8,052	10,192	13,080	16,061	18,354	20,717	78,404	126.6	128.3	122.8	114.3	112.9	257.3
Of which:													
(a) Basic capital	7,112	8,612	10,836	13,115	14,896	17,142	64,601	121.1	125.8	121.0	113.6	115.1	241.0

TABLE X —*Continued*

Including:													
1. Industry (including industrial housing)	1,672	2,091	2,845	3,451	3,796	4,170	16,353	125.1	136.1	121.3	110.0	109.9	249.4
Of which, industries regulated by the Supreme Council of National Economy	1,318	1,659	2,331	2,880	3,165	3,465	13,500	125.9	140.5	123.6	109.9	109.5	262.9
2. Electrification not including factory power plants	284	332	453	656	757	861	3,059	116.9	136.4	144.8	115.4	113.7	303.2
3. Agriculture	3,084	3,664	4,173	4,720	5,079	5,516	23,152	118.8	113.9	113.1	107.6	108.6	178.8
4. Transportation	896	1,128	1,497	1,878	2,394	3,105	10,002	125.9	132.7	125.5	127.5	129.7	346.5
(b) Operating capital	940	1,580	2,244	2,946	3,458	3,575	13,803	168.1	142.0	131.3	117.4	103.4	380.3
V. Government budget, central and local, net expenditures	5,879	7,123	8,633	10,120	11,810	13,669	51,355	121.3	121.2	117.2	116.7	115.7	232.5
Of which:													
(a) General administration and defense	1,751	1,878	1,991	2,195	2,406	2,716	11,186	107.1	106.0	110.2	109.6	112.9	155.1
(b) Social welfare and cultural activities	1,238	1,450	1,769	2,167	2,566	2,994	10,946	117.1	122.0	122.5	118.4	116.7	241.8
(c) Financing of national economy	2,424	3,284	4,204	5,058	6,081	6,981	25,608	136.0	128.0	120.3	120.2	114.8	288.0
(d) All other	464	511	669	700	757	978	3,615	110.1	130.9	104.6	108.1	129.2	209.9

APPENDIX III

EXPLANATORY NOTES

Weights and Measures:

Kilogram	2.2046 lbs.
Centner	220.46 lbs.
Metric Ton	2,204.6 lbs.
Meter	39.37 inches.
Kilometer	0.621 miles.
Square Meter	10.764 square feet.
Hectare	2.471 acres.

Ruble .... equals 51½ cents.

Supreme Council of National Economy (S.C.N.E.)	Central government department in charge of state industry.
Census Industry	Industrial establishments employing 15 workers or more and using mechanical power or establishments where no mechanical power is used but at least 30 workers are employed.
Soviet fiscal year	October 1-September 30.
Soviet agricultural year	July 1-June 30.

APPENDIX IV

SOVIET-AMERICAN TRADE

Soviet-American trade, which in 1929 entered its sixth year, amounted for the period ending July 31, 1929, to over half a billion dollars. This sum, constituting about 15 per cent of the total Soviet foreign trade since 1924, includes the export and import operations of the Amtorg Trading Corporation, representing the principal industrial and trading organizations of the Soviet Union, as well as of the All-Russian Textile Syndicate, which purchases cotton for the Soviet textile industry, Centrosoyus and Selskosojus, representing Soviet consumers' and agricultural cooperatives respectively, and the Amkino Corporation, which distributes the films of Sovkino and other Soviet moving picture producing organizations. All of these companies have been incorporated under the laws of the state of New York. Included in the total are also the shipments of Soviet manganese to the United States and the imports of furs by American firms having special agreements with Soviet organizations. The share of the Amtorg Trading Corporation alone in this turnover amounted to about $215,000,000, the Amtorg handling the bulk of general imports and practically all the exports of machinery for industrial, agricultural and transportation purposes, as well as exports of certain raw materials such as non-ferrous metals, rubber and chemicals and of hundreds of miscellaneous products.

Of the $540,000,000 which represents the turnover of Soviet-American trade since 1924, purchases in the United States made up $430,000,000 and sales of Soviet products in this country $110,000,000. Large unfavorable trade balances were reported each year, and the adverse balance against the U.S.S.R. for the entire period aggregated about $320,000,000. The Soviet Union has a favorable trade balance with most of the other countries with which it does business.

Soviet purchases in the United States have been growing at a steady rate, with exception being made for the year 1924-25, in which year exports from this country reached an unusually high figure, due primarily to the purchase of over $20,000,000 worth of flour—an emergency purchase necessitated by the failure of crops in the Soviet Union. No such purchases have been made since that year. Omitting the fiscal year 1924-25, when Soviet purchases in this country totaled $86,938,000, the following totals for Soviet purchases in the United States are obtained:

1923-24	$43,916,000
1925-26	48,560,000
1926-27	71,689,000
1927-28	91,232,000
1928-29 (10 months) ....approximately	84,000,000

In the ten months beginning October 1, 1928, orders for the U.S.S.R. to a total value of $51,000,000 were placed in this country by the Amtorg Trading Corporation alone, as compared with $33,000,000 for the entire preceding year. A new record for Soviet-American trade is expected this year.

The greater part of the purchases in this country for the past years was made up of cotton. Purchases by the Textile Syndicate since its inauguration in December, 1923, up to July, 1929, amounted to about $245,000,000. Scores of ships have been chartered to bring American cotton to the Soviet port of Murmansk on the Arctic coast and to other Soviet ports in the north and on the Black Sea.

By far the most rapid growth, among the various groups of commodities purchased in the United States for the Soviet Union, has been shown by machinery and apparatus, including industrial machinery, agricultural implements, automotive equipment, transportation and electrical machinery. Purchases of industrial machinery by the Amtorg Trading Corporation alone, which amounted to $2,500,000 in the fiscal year 1926-27, exceeded $11,000,000 in 1927-28 and amounted to $23,200,000 for the ten months ending July 31, 1929. There are dozens of Soviet industries which enter the American market every year to make purchases of machinery.

Imports of agricultural equipment, principally tractors, have shown a large increase, due to the expansion of large-scale farming in the U.S.S.R. Agricultural equipment purchases for the ten months ending July 31,

1929, amounted to $21,000,000, one-third more than the purchases of the preceding year, and three times the purchases of two years previous.

An important factor in Soviet-American economic relations are the contracts for technical assistance, largely in the construction of new industrial enterprises in the Soviet Union, which have been concluded within the past two years with important American engineering and manufacturing companies. A list of such contracts is given below.

The bulk of the purchases now being made in this country for the Soviet Union involve credit terms. Large-scale credits, some up to a period of five years, are being granted by an increasing number of concerns, including the International General Electric Company, the Westinghouse Electric International Company, the International Combustion Engineering Corporation, International Harvester Company, John Deere Company, Allis-Chalmers Company, Worthington Pump Company, Ingersoll-Rand Company, Link Belt Company, Caterpillar Tractor Company, the Hercules Motor Company, and others.

Sales of Soviet products in this country have not shown a growth comparable with that of purchases. In the past three years (1926, 1927, 1928) sales in this country have amounted to 24, 21, and 22 million dollars respectively. The market for Soviet products in this country has been confined to about a score of items, including bristles, casings, furs, poultry, mushrooms, seeds, candy, flax, crude drugs, manganese ore, precious metals, handicraft products, and small quantities of lumber and coal.

Mention should also be made of the contracts concluded by the Soviet Naphtha Syndicate with the Standard Oil Company of New York and the Vacuum Oil Company, calling for the delivery of Soviet oil products, to the value of $10,000,000 annually, to the far and near eastern markets of these companies.

TECHNICAL ASSISTANCE CONTRACTS CONCLUDED BY SOVIET ORGANIZATIONS WITH AMERICAN FIRMS AND INDIVIDUALS

(List as of August 15, 1929)

Hugh L. Cooper and Company—Consulting engineers on the construction of the Dnieper hydro-electric power plant in the Ukraine.

Stuart, James and Cooke—Consulting engineers for the Donugol Coal Trust, the Southern Steel Trust (coal mines), the Moscow Coal Trust and the Kizel Coal Trust; making plans for the opening of new mines, rebuilding of old mines and installation of modern equipment.

Freyn Engineering Company—Consulting engineers on the designing of steel mills to be constructed in various parts of the country.

Radio Corporation of America—Exchange of patents

and technical information with the Soviet Weak Current Trust; technical assistance in the manufacture of radio apparatus in the U.S.S.R.

International General Electric Company—Technical assistance in the Soviet electrical industry and exchange of patent and other technical information with the Soviet State Electrotechnical Trust.

Sperry Gyroscope Company—Technical assistance in the manufacture of marine instruments.

Nitrogen Engineering Company—Technical assistance in constructing and operating a $10,000,000 ammonia fertilizer factory.

Du Pont de Nemours and Company—Technical assistance in erecting fertilizer factories.

Longacre Engineering and Construction Company—Technical assistance and supervision of construction of apartment houses and public buildings in Moscow.

Arthur P. Davis, Lyman Bishop—Consulting engineers on the irrigation projects of the "Sredazvodkhoz" (Central Asiatic Water Economy) in Soviet Central Asia.

The McCormick Company—Designing of the largest Soviet baking plant in Moscow.

Albert Kahn, Inc.—Designing of buildings for the Stalingrad Tractor factory, to produce 40,000 tractors per year.

Harry D. Gibbs—Technical cooperation in Soviet aniline industry.

Frank D. Chase, Inc.—Technical assistance in the foundry industry.

Ford Motor Company—Technical assistance in the construction and operation of an automobile factory to produce 100,000 cars per year.

Taft Pierce Co.—Technical assistance in the foundry industry.

Archer E. Wheeler—Consulting engineer in Soviet copper industry.

C. F. Seabrook Co.—Technical advisors on road-building in the Moscow province.

Foster-Wheeler Corp.—Technical assistance in the Soviet oil refining industry.

Lockwood Greene & Company—Technical assistance in the reorganization and reconstruction of existing textile mills and in the design and construction of new plants.

Roberts and Schaefer Company—Technical assistance to the Donetz Coal Trust.

Arthur J. Brandt—Reconstruction of the Moscow Amo Automobile plant to a production, in one shift, of 25,000 cars per annum.

Hercules Motor Company—Assistance in the production of engines for heavy trucks in the Yaroslavl plant.

Newport News Shipbuilding and Drydock Company—Technical assistance in the construction of turbines.

Seiberling Rubber Company—Designing and assistance in construction of a rubber tire plant at Yaroslavl.

INDICATORS OF NATIONAL

(PROGRAM AND

I. LABOR, AVERAGE NUMBER OF PERSONS WORKING FOR HIRE, INCLUDING AGRICULTURAL PURSUITS, in thousand persons..............

II. NATIONAL INCOME, in million rubles—
1. In prices of each year..
2. In prices of 1926-27...

III. CAPITAL INVESTMENTS IN BASIC FUNDS OF SOCIALIZED SECTOR OF NATIONAL ECONOMY, in million rubles, at prices of each year.......

IV. ELECTRIFICATION—
1. Capacity at end of year, excluding industrial power plants, in thousand kilowatts ....
Regional public utility plants..............................
2. Production of power, excluding industrial plants, in million kilowatt-hours...
Regional plants, in million kilowatt-hours..........................
3. Capital investments, excluding industrial power plants, in million rubles in prices of each year...

V. INDUSTRY—
A. All industry—
1. Gross output, in million rubles, at prices of 1926-27 ....
Census industry ....
Small-scale industry, including milling..............................
2. Gross output, in million rubles, at prices of respective years..........
Census industry ....
Small-scale industry, including milling..............................
B. Industry under supervision of Supreme Economic Council—
1. Gross production, in million rubles, at prices of 1926-27.................
Producers' goods industries ....
Consumers' goods industries ....
2. Number of workers, in thousands......................................
3. Value of annual production per worker, in rubles, at prices of 1926-27......
4. Production costs (1927-28 = 100)...................................
5. Capital investments, in million rubles, at prices of each year..............
Producers' goods industries ....
Consumers' good industries ....
Miscellaneous ....

VI. AGRICULTURE—
1. Gross production, in million rubles, at prices of 1926-27 ‡ ....
2. Machinery supplied, in million rubles ....
3. Tractors supplied, in thousand 10-h.p. units..............................
4. Consumption of mineral fertilizer, except lime and oil-cake flour, in thousand tons ....
5. Capital investments in socialized sector, in million rubles, at prices of each year

VII. TRANSPORTATION—
1. Freight operation of railways, in billion ton-kilometers..................
2. Revenue of railways, in million rubles...................................
3. Capital investments, in prices of each year, in million rubles..............
Railways ....

VIII. BUDGET, in million rubles—
1. Federal revenue..
2. Financing, in federal budget..
Industry ....
Electrification ....
Transportation ....
Agriculture (except expenditures on budget of Commissariat for Agriculture) ....
Irrigation ....
Miscellaneous ....

IX. INDEXES (1913 = 100)—
1. Producers' prices, industrial products.....................................
2. Prices paid by marketing agencies for agricultural products...............
Grain ....
Industrial crops..
Animal products..
3. Cost of living index..

* The figures in this table differ somewhat from those given elsewhere (particularly for estimated according to the methods used in the Five-Year Plan. These methods have been

† Percentages are estimated on the basis of exact not rounded figures as given here.

ECONOMY, 1927-28 TO 1929-30 *

ACTUAL RESULTS)

1927-28,	1928-29		1929-30		Per Cent of Preceding Year †			
				Revised	1928-29		1929-30	Revised
Actual	5-yr. Plan	Actual	5-yr. Plan	Program	5-yr. Plan	Actual	5-yr. Plan	Program
11,456	11,901	12,150	12,793	13,293	104.9	106.1	107.5	109.4
24,681	27,469	29,222	30,884	33,079	111.3	118.4	112.4	113.2
24,429	27,031	27,458	31,299	33,059	110.7	112.4	115.8	120.4
4,042	5,270	5,560	7,414	10,008	....	137.6	140.7	180.0
868	1,008	1,060	.....	1,631	114.0	122.1	....	153.9
528	603	662	.....	1,160	116.0	125.4	....	175.2
2,503	3,248	3,225	.....	4,693	135.8	128.8	....	145.5
1,814	2,415	2,400	.....	3,706	129.1	132.3	....	154.4
269	332	369	453	614	116.9	137.2	136.4	166.4
19,093	21,164	22,292	25,009	28,050	115.6	116.8	118.2	125.8
14,131	16,439	17,115	19,885	22,497	118.4	121.1	121.0	131.4
4,962	4,725	5,177	5,124	5,553	106.7	104.3	108.4	107.3
18,314	20,358	21,401	23,081	26,406	113.4	116.9	113.4	123.4
13,566	15,646	16,416	18,097	21,108	115.7	121.0	115.7	128.6
4,748	4,712	4,985	4,984	5,298	106.4	105.0	105.8	106.3
11,067	13,246	13,698	16,091	18,092	121.4	123.7	121.5	132.1
4,663	5,516	6,052	6,960	8,782	125.6	129.8	126.2	145.1
6,404	7,730	7,641	9,131	9,310	118.6	119.3	118.1	121.9
2,132	2,194	2,298	2,280	2,430	104.3	107.8	104.1	105.7
5,190	6,037	5,957	7,060	7,446	116.4	114.8	117.0	125.0
100.0	93.0	95.0	86.0	84.5	93.0	95.0	92.5	89.0
1,825	1,659	1,679	2,331	3,267	125.9	126.7	140.5	194.6
950	1,224	1,239	1,738	2,489	130.5	130.4	142.0	200.9
365	363	363	482	472	99.5	99.5	132.8	130.0
10	72	77	111	306	....	770.0	154.0	397.0
14,526	15,087	14,787	16,303	15,186	103.5	101.8	108.4	102.7
149	220	220	304	406	147.7	147.7	138.2	184.5
3.3	9.7	9.7	25.0	41.0§	290.1	290.1	258.8	422.7
216	558	428	1,776	1,066	215.4	198.1	318.3	248.8
243	611	664	1,049	1,636	....	273.2	171.7	246.4
88.2	97.0	106.7	108.7	127.0	110.1	121.0	112.1	119.0
1,730	1,830	2,025	2,095	2,439	112.4	117.1	114.5	120.4
943	1,101	1,205	1,430	1,840	124.3	127.8	129.9	152.7
757	844	942	1,087	1,335	118.2	124.4	128.8	141.7
6,836	7,752	8,103	9,178	11,261	115.4	118.5	118.4	139.0
1,959	2,705	2,809	3,310	4,813	139.2	143.4	122.4	171.3
659	945	986	1,090	1,789	145.1	149.6	115.3	181.4
135	184	175	225	310	135.9	129.6	122.3	177.1
535	732	770	1,018	1,244	131.4	143.9	139.1	161.6
161	335	350	358	618	210.7	217.4	105.4	176.6
35.5	40	39	65	110	109.3	109.9	162.6	282.1
423.5	469	489	559	742	....	115.0	119.0	152.0
185.3	182.7	184.8	174.7	180.2	98.6	99.7	95.6	97.5
156.4	165.0	183.3	164.2	178.8	105.5	117.2	99.5	97.5
134.6	156.6	190.4	155.4	180.6	116.3	141.5	99.2	94.9
139.8	144.6	146.0	144.6	146.2	103.4	104.4	100.0	100.1
181.8	183.4	197.6	183.0	198.7	100.9	108.7	99.8	100.6
199.9	205.5	209.7	200.4	204.5	102.8	104.9	97.5	97.5

national income and agricultural production), since for the purposes of comparison they are slightly revised.

‡ Crops are for 1927, 1928 and 1929.

§ The figure for tractors supplied has been raised to 54,000 units.

For Product Safety Concerns and Information please contact our EU
representative GPSR@taylorandfrancis.com
Taylor & Francis Verlag GmbH, Kaufingerstraße 24, 80331 München, Germany

www.ingramcontent.com/pod-product-compliance
Ingram Content Group UK Ltd.
Pitfield, Milton Keynes, MK11 3LW, UK
UKHW021505240926
475702UK00035B/435

9781032486345